Sensing the Spirit

Sensing the Spirit

Toward the Future of Religious Life

Judith A. Merkle SNDdeN

t&tclark

LONDON • NEW YORK • OXFORD • NEW DELHI • SYDNEY

T&T CLARK
Bloomsbury Publishing Plc
50 Bedford Square, London, WC1B 3DP, UK
1385 Broadway, New York, NY 10018, USA
29 Earlsfort Terrace, Dublin 2, Ireland

BLOOMSBURY, T&T CLARK and the T&T Clark logo are trademarks of
Bloomsbury Publishing Plc

First published in Great Britain 2023

A catalogue record for this book is available from the British Library.

A catalog record for this book is available from the Library of Congress.

ISBN: HB: 978-0-5677-0700-0
PB: 978-0-5677-0699-7
ePDF: 978-0-5677-0702-4
ePUB: 978-0-5677-0701-7

Typeset by Deanta Global Publishing Services, Chennai, India
Printed and bound in Great Britain

To find out more about our authors and books visit www.bloomsbury.com and
sign up for our newsletters.

In gratitude to the women and men
who are on the journey of
religious life in our time.
May we move forward to sense the Spirit
with courage and wisdom.

In loving memory of my aunt:
Ann Catherine Merkle CPPS (1923–2018)

CONTENTS

DOCUMENTS CITED AND ABBREVIATIONS USED[1]

Lumen Gentium: Dogmatic Constitution on the Church (Vatican II, 1964)	LG
Dignitatis Humanae: Declaration on Religious Freedom (Vatican II, 1965)	DH
Gaudium et Spes: Pastoral Constitution on the Church in the Modern World (Vatican II, 1965)	GS
Apostolicam Actuousitatem: Decree on the Apostolate of the Laity (Vatican II, 1965)	AA
Justice in the World (Synod of Bishops, 1971)	JW
Redemptor Hominis: Christ the Redeemer (John Paul II, 1979)[2]	RH
Dives in Misericordia: On the Mercy of God (John Paul II, 1980)	DM
Sollicitudo Rei Socialis: On Social Concern (John Paul II, 1987)[3]	SRS

---

[1]*The Documents of Vatican II*, ed. Walter M. Abbott, S.J. (New York: Herder and Herder, 1966).

[2]*The Encyclicals of John Paul II*, ed. and intro. J. Michael Miller, C.S.B. (Huntington, IN: Our Sunday Vistor, 1996).

[3]All social encyclicals are cited from *Catholic Social Thought: The Documentary Heritage*, ed. David J. O'Brien and Thomas A. Shannon (Maryknoll, NY: Orbis, 2002).

---

[4]Benedict XVI, *Caritas in Veritate* (Vatican City, *Liberia Editrice Vaticana*, 2009).
[5]Francis, *Evangelii Gaudium* (Vatican City, *Liberia Editrice Vaticana*, 2013).
[6]Francis, *Laudato Si'* (Vatican City, *Liberia Editrice Vaticana*, 2015).
[7]Francis, *Amoris Laetitia* (Vatican City, *Liberia Editrice Vaticana*, 2016).
[8]Francis, *Gaudete et exsultate* (Vatican City, *Liberia Editrice Vaticana*, 2018).
[9]Francis, *Fratelli Tutti* (Vatican City, *Liberia Editrice Vaticana*, 2020).
[10]Francis, *La Querida Amazonia* (Vatican City, *Liberia Editrice Vaticana*, 2020).

Introduction

The way forward for religious congregations today is unclear. To suggest that religious congregations should be about "sensing the Spirit" is a risky proposition. While there has been a widespread affirmation in the history of Christianity that God is present in our lives through the power of the Holy Spirit, to attempt to indicate how the Spirit acts, or where the Spirit is, is hazardous.

Religious refer to the presence of the Spirit daily. Most religious testify that their lives are changed through the action of the Spirit. Their founding is attributed to the Spirit working in and through the founder or foundress. Decisions at times of crisis are chronicled as being led by the Spirit. Daily community life validates that people do change their life orientation and adopt life standards which are markers of the Spirit: love, joy, peace, patience, generosity, goodness, trust, gentleness, and self-control (Gal. 5:22). Religious find the Spirit's presence in their own growth and development and find no problem in identifying the action of the Spirit in this very personal aspect of their lives. Yet to assume the Spirit has anything to do with the crisis facing religious congregations today might be met with objections.

Those who recognize the challenge of aging populations, decline in entrants, lack of personnel to staff long-standing ministries, and financial limitations may dispute the suggestion that the Spirit is a suitable resource to consult. Too much "Spirit" breeds irrationality and dreaming, which leaves untouched the hard realities that must be faced. Memories of congregational decisions attributed to the Spirit, which appeared to lack good information, democratic processes, or reasoned examination of alternatives, linger in members' minds. Other religious recall encounters with individuals who "discerned" decisions which were "not to be questioned," which causes them to wonder just how the freedom of the Spirit was present. These experiences raise concerns about the meaning of discernment, and how to separate true discernment from its counterfeits. Decisions "of the Spirit" mark them with a sacred aura they might not deserve. Talk of the Spirit devalues the concrete, and the material, which makes a good banker better suited to the times, some charge. Lastly, the tangibility of the Spirit seems nebulous. Isn't what the Spirit wants already our own yearnings and potentials? Should we not just put our heads together and decide, and leave the Spirit for personal prayer?

To consider religious life today requires one to recognize that there is a tension between its theological mystery and the challenges it faces. Religious life is often considered in the abstract, yet it is lived concretely in defined sociological contexts. At first glance, it might seem that its theological reality stands in the way of dealing effectively with the concrete facts it must embrace. Yet the opposite will be presented in this writing.

This book will assume that the Spirit is a source of freedom and guidance for religious congregations today. The Spirit is neither far from our own planning, nor from consultation with people with skills important to a decision. Yet asking the question of what difference the Spirit makes in the process is important. People of faith know the marks of true discernment are characteristic of those which scripture indicates are signs of the Spirit in the life of a disciple (2 Cor. 4:7-15). Decisions of the Spirit reflect the following of Christ in the gospel. They embrace recognized norms and are not self-serving. Their outcomes offer a love which edifies others. Seeking the Spirit involves an acceptance of adversity and patient acceptance of our own transformation, conversion, and need for both. Lastly, these decisions reflect a quality of life which reflects the kind of heart which is in tune with goodness.[1]

Christian discernment focuses on Jesus Christ as the self-expression of God in history. This is Jesus who is more than a moral ideal; it is Jesus Christ who is the source of our salvation.[2] Jesus emptied himself in death on the cross (Phil. 2) and was raised by the Spirit (Rom. 8:11). The Spirit is both the Spirit of Jesus and of the

[1]This is a paraphrase of comments by Yves Congar O.P., *Spirit of God: Short Writings on the Holy Spirit* (Washington, DC: The Catholic University of America Press, 2018), 29ff.
[2]Judith A. Merkle, *Discipleship, Secularity and the Modern Self: Dancing to Silent Music* (London: T&T Clark/Bloomsbury, 2020), Chapter 5. See also: Elizabeth Johnson, "Christ Died for Us," in *Abounding in Kindness* (New York: Orbis Books, 2015).

Father: the Spirit of the One who raises Jesus to life; the Spirit of Jesus who receives life in the full. The life of the Spirit is a paradigm of the way forward for religious today. Religious are to both give and receive life as the way to share in the life of the Trinity, in the Spirit, and move to the future. Religious know the emptying of Christ in the letting go which recent times have required. Yet the Spirit is also at the Source of the new life to which religious are called, in and for the world. The Spirit we desire through Christ continues God's action of healing and creating in history, in congregational life and in society. The Spirit does more than merely inspire certain distinctive actions: the Spirit transforms our very being, thereby establishing us in a new relationship with God (Rom. 8: 14-16).[3] The Spirit is the source of the new life needed for the future of religious life, and the guidance for the concrete decisions it must embrace.

As religious seek to "sense the Spirit" to engage the challenges of today they can rely on the vision of Vatican II that the Spirit is with us in our times and in the church. "Christ is now at work in the hearts of men and women through the energy of the Spirit. He not only arouses a desire for the age to come, but also vivifies, purifies, and strengthens those generous impulses by which the human family strives to render its life more human and to submit the whole earth to this goal" (GS 38).

This book is not a full theology of the Holy Spirit nor commentary on the advances in pneumatology which mark the church. It will assume that the future of religious congregations depends on a new "reading the signs of the times,"—Vatican II's naming of attention to the movement of Spirit, as well as Spirit of the Synod in the church today. An underlying theme of the text is a recognition of secularity as a sign of the times and as a new context of religious life. This book will assume there is no uniform answer to the forward movement of religious congregations. In the Spirit, unity is always in dynamic counterplay with differentiation.[4] A unity of forward movement cannot be imposed, nor can differences between cultures of religious

[3]Robert P. Imbelli, "Holy Spirit," in *The New Dictionary of Theology*, ed. Joseph A. Komonchak et al. (Wilmington, DL: Michael Glazier, 1989), 474–89.
[4]Mary Frohlich RSCJ, *Breathed into Wholeness: Catholicity and Life in the Spirit* (New York: Orbis Books, 2019), 204.

congregations be overlooked and ignored. Rather, the text will treat issues which are universal enough to be interpreted by many, yet sufficiently concrete to capture matters beyond the surface.

Part I addresses the foundations of this study. Chapter 1 will present religious life as an "Unfolding Seed." It will introduce the thought of Charles Taylor on the meaning of the secular age. It will indicate that conditions of secularity, the significance of the Reign of God, charism, and shifts in theology since Vatican II interface in decisions regarding the future of religious congregations. Chapter 2, "The Niche of Religious Life," will draw on the environmental concept of niche to explore the changed conditions of religious life and its ministry, and ask their implications for the way forward. Chapter 3, "Beyond Survival," will unpack an environmental study as an analogy for a process of transformation for congregations for the future. It will focus on constants in religious life throughout the centuries which can stabilize and generate new life in changing circumstances.

Part II, "Toward the Future of Religious Life," addresses issues which affect the future of religious life. Chapter 4, "The Vows in Secular Culture," will focus on the vows in general as a framework or style of the Christian life.[5] It will discuss the vows in terms of the Vatican II insistence that being a man or woman for God involves being one who is for the world and ready to take responsibility for its concerns. Vows will be understood in their relationship to authentic becoming, standing with the People of God and their needs, and developing a primary capacity for God. It will address the role of conversion in the lives of all believers and its role in the lives of religious. Chapter 5, "Adult Christian Living in Secular Culture," will address the crisis of institutions in all adult vocations in the church. It will outline spiritual hungers which exist in secular society and how they impact religious congregations. Chapter 6, "Adaptations for a New Environment," will look again to nature for how life changes beyond, death, extinction, and demise. Adaptations flow from meeting the challenges that confront religious life as it engages a secular world. It will suggest how the gifts of

---

[5]This approach is in place of a consideration of each vow in new circumstances, which will follow in Part II of this project.

faith, hope, and love address the doubt, uncertainty, and fear which impact the decisions facing religious in these times.

It is hoped that the weaving together of these selected insights might offer insight into the meaning of "sensing the Spirit" for religious congregations today. This is not a book of solutions, management techniques, or quick fixes. It is an investigation and reflection which offers tools for religious and their congregations as they make decisions for their future. Men and women religious hopefully will add to these insights those which arise from their own contexts. This book offers a framework, to be adapted, whose intent is to support religious and future religious to identify how the Spirit is leading them.

I would like to thank my own religious community, Sisters of Notre Dame de Namur, an international congregation of Catholic religious sisters and associates for the many ways it nurtures my own life as a religious and witnesses to the ongoing challenges outlined in this book. Niagara University research council, my colleagues in the Religious Studies Department and the library staff have provided both financial and collegial support in the writing of this book. I am indebted to Anna Turton, Sinead O'Connor, and the Bloomsbury/T&T Clark staff for their careful attention to this text. I am thankful to the Lay Centre in Rome, its director Donna Orsuto, and its students for their hospitality during my research period there. I am grateful to my colleagues in the Catholic Theological Society of America and to my family and friends, for the unique ways each supports my life, which would not flourish without them.

PART I

Foundations

1

The Unfolding Seed

The Gospel of Mark portrays Jesus speaking of the Kingdom. "With what can we compare the kingdom of God, or what parable will we use for it? It is like a mustard seed, which, when sown upon the ground, is the smallest of all the seeds on earth; yet when it is sown it grows up and becomes the greatest of all shrubs, and puts forth large branches, so that the birds of the air can make nests in its shade" (Mark 4:30). We wonder, as we ponder the future of religious life in a secular age, whether a scriptural image can have any impact on how to proceed? We know how to create a five-year plan, to form a committee, and to raise funds for our projects. Yet today we sense we are being invited to something more. This "more" is outside our comfort zone to the degree our ordinary plans do not meet it. We ask: just how can we nurture the seeds of life among us and foster the future of religious life?

After Vatican II, religious recognized the need to update their structures, change outdated practices, and set new goals for their ministry. We assumed these changes would modernize our congregations as well as attract new members. Our day-to-day practices were adapted to the realities of modern living. We became less enclosed and provided more personal freedom of choice both in the spiritual life and in daily living. Yet we have found that these changes have not drawn people to religious life as we expected. The fixing and improving helped to heal the restrictions of outdated practice. But the changes we made were not universally shared and appreciated by all, nor did they attract new members. Over time, a sense of disappointment, negativity associated with scandals in the church, and conflicting expectations among members impacted our sense of moving forward together. The differences—theological, generational, and cultural—among members make it difficult to form a basic consensus upon which to move ahead. When we find it hard to discuss and accept differences among us, we drift into nostalgia and vague spiritual platitudes. While there are many positives among us as congregations, these concerns juxtapose those accomplishments. It is neither easy to ignore these experiences nor explain them away. They disturb us with the reality that we need a new approach. What might the parable of the mustard seed address in this dilemma?

Theologian Hans Urs von Balthasar offers a comment which touches on this situation. He states, "The Church since the Council has to a large extent put off her mystical characteristics," he goes on, "she has become a Church of permanent conversations, organizations, advisory committees, congresses, synods, commissions, academics, parties, pressure groups, functions, structures and restructurings, sociological experiments, statistics . . ."[1] As religious, we recognize his point, as we have given quite a bit of energy to these endeavors. The heart of his comment focuses on the need to place more attention on the grounding of our life, amid all we seek to build in church and society. Sociologist Patricia Wittberg SC puts social scientific flesh on von Balthasar's observations. She remarks that changes since Vatican II have led to an absence of an internally coherent group spirituality in congregations which causes religious to struggle to link their own personal spiritualities to each other and to connect their work and their religious vocations.[2] In different ways, von Balthasar and Wittberg call for religious to attend to the deeper grounding of their lives. This does not suggest the abandonment of ministries or withdrawal from society. Jesuit Peter Bisson indicates what attention to grounding suggests. After a post-conciliar Jesuit congregation, he stated: it is not simply a matter of the society's "reflecting on the quality of its engagement with the world, but on the quality of its engagement with Christ actively engaged in

[1]Hans Urs von Balthasar, *Elucidations*, trans. John Riches (San Francisco, CA: Ignatius Press, 1998), 109–10.
[2]Sociologist Patricia Wittberg comments on the vacuum left by the dissolution of institutionally based religious life which gets resolved by borrowing identities from other groups in society. See: Patricia Wittberg, *From Piety to Professionalism and Back? Transformations of Organized Religious Virtuosity* (Lanham, MD: Lexington Books, 2006), 265.

the world."[3] Both Balthasar's reference to mysticism and Wittberg's assessment of the need for a coherent spirituality call for a renewed posture of "contemplation in action" in religious life.

The Parable of the Mustard Seed and Religious

The parable of the mustard seed touches on this deeper reality in religious life. Gerhard Lohfink, in *The Forty Parables of Jesus*, examines the parable itself.[4] Jesus' announcement of the now-inbreaking of the Reign of God met with immediate opposition. People around him experienced the same old problems, occupation by the Romans, sickness, and poverty. They objected to Jesus: where is the change in the world which you are talking about? They expected the coming of the Reign of God would mean something dramatic, throwing off the Romans, things changing in an instant. Without these real changes, Jesus' message seemed empty.

Might religious today offer this same objection to the coming of the Kingdom? Religious wonder what happened, is this all there is? According to the sister formation ideas of post-Vatican II, religious were to be leaders. Members ask, where are they? Did we not build larger houses of formation to accommodate all the vocations? Clerical orders and most congregations barely can offer a skeleton service to existing institutions because of aging populations. What does the parable say to these anxieties?

Lohfink clarifies Jesus does not compare the Reign of God to a mustard seed; rather the parable testifies to the whole process by which a very small seed becomes a great shrub. The parable does not speak of the Reign of God in static terms but rather of its coming. Lohfink explains, "this is about the dynamics of the reign of God."[5] The parable affirms that, at present, the Reign of God

---

[3]Peter Bisson, "The Post Conciliar Jesuit Congregations: Social Commitment Constructing a New World of Religious Meaning," *Lonergan Workshop* 19 (2007): 1–35 at 32.
[4]Gerard Lohfink, *The Forty Parables of Jesus*, trans. Linda M. Mahoney (Collegeville, MN: Liturgical Press, 2021), 56–63.
[5]Ibid., 58.

can seem much in the background, unimpressive, overlooked, and dismissed as irrelevant. But it is unfolding, gaining strength, and becoming so rooted in the soil in this time and place; that the birds of the air rest in its shade.

The shrub which grows in the parable refers to a world in the literature of the ancient Near East, where the power of kings themselves with their kingdoms and empires are depicted as a giant cedar in whose shade many living things, including the birds of the air, dwell. It was clear to Jesus that the Reign of God had nothing to do with the imperial claims of the rulers of his age and that of Hellenistic ideology. Jesus clarifies that the Reign of God is not just an idea. Like the mustard seed, the Reign of God must be planted somewhere: in the hearts of a concrete people; embedded in concrete circumstances. The parable testifies that *in this hour*, the Reign of God is as insignificant as a mustard seed, and the true People of God but a tiny flock (Luke 12:32), but from this obscure beginning a new thing, a different thing, is already growing. It is growing toward an all-encompassing realm, a new world community. This is as certain to come about as that from a tiny mustard seed a giant shrub arises. Perhaps as religious listen to this parable it may take their imaginations beyond the renewal of fixing and improving they accomplished after Vatican II, to an openness to the idea that there still can be more. What difference might another type of renewal make—that of unfolding and deepening?

Toward an Evolutionary Image

When Jesus offered the parable of the mustard seed, he was likely at a botanical level referring to the black mustard (*brassica nigra*) whose seeds are usually small but could grow from five to nine feet on the shores of the Sea of Galilee.[6] As Jesus looked to nature for images of spiritual realities, we look there today. Evolutionary studies reveal that the nature we encounter in our world represents only 1 percent of the species which have existed. In other words,

---

[6]Ibid.

99 percent of the species that have ever lived are now extinct.[7] Even what we encounter as a natural reality is only a sliver of what has existed on this earth. The process of growth affirmed by the parable is deepened by the evolutionary facts that growth involves death as well as developing life over time. It seems fair to draw from the analogy that the religious life which we have known in the last one to two hundred years is not its only expression, but part of a response of fidelity which has gone before. Beneath the set patterns we have experienced, there is a deeper energy of life response which has transformed lives, built institutions, and engaged societies in a manner which has enriched the People of God. That life continues today and will continue.

The parable suggests that in God's time religious life is part of the unfolding seed of the Reign of God. It is a result of God's work and ours, yet we are just one stage in this larger process. There is no way to map where we are on our journey, as its mystery is beyond us, but it does seem possible to mark significant elements which impact the moment of which we are a part. First, we live in a secular age. What we mean by secularity and how we understand its impact is important. Second, we know "the Reign of God in our midst" and we also recognize its presence in our congregational charism. Key to our future is our interpretation of our charism and how the Spirit is acting among us as religious. Third, we are conscious that we live in times of great transition in the church and society. Understanding of the Christian life has changed. The theological shifts of Vatican II and beyond impact religious life, its relationship to society, and many other areas. These challenges facing religious will be addressed in the following and throughout the text. We do this remembering that Vatican II encouraged the church not only to *aggiormento*, to renewal, but *ressourcement*, to retrieve elements of the faith of the church life to express them meaningfully in new times. Both postures of renewal will serve us as we explore their relevance to our search.

---

[7]Terrence P. Ehrman, C.S.C, "Ecology: The Science of Interconnections," in *The Theological and Ecological Vision of Laudato Si: Everything is Connected*, ed. Vincent J. Miller (London: Bloomsbury/T&T Clark, 2017), 51–73 at 52.

The Secular Age

Charles Taylor, a Canadian philosopher, reminds us that the "background" for modern life has changed. Background refers to the context of our lives, beliefs, and outlooks which we take for granted and seldom formulate into clear terms.[8] Similar to a cluster of ideas or worldview, the background is unconscious. Yet it forms the framework by which we interpret our experience, frame the conditions of experience, and answer the spiritual and moral questions of our times. Taylor argues that today this background is marked by the experience of the secular. In contrast to people who lived five hundred years ago, we come to belief or assume a posture of unbelief using a new set of conditions marked by secularity.

There are three indicators of secularity in modern experience. One: we live in societies where public space is emptied of the mention of God. Two: we notice around us the falling off of religious belief. Most importantly, three: the conditions of coming to belief have drastically changed. In contrast to a former age when it was difficult not to believe in God, we come to belief in a climate where belief in God is one option among others to explain the integrity of life. While there have always been rival theories to the existence of God and the meaning of life, modern living brings us side-by-side with people who have very different interpretations of the same life. That which brings meaning to the life of a believer is absent in their lives.[9]

At the same time, in modern society people assume a separation of what is of public interest, such as the political activity of citizens, and the private sphere of personal interest. In this sphere religion is a private interest and adherence to it is seen as one option among many. The decline, and eventual elimination, of religion is imagined as a type of subtraction theory in societal life: as modernization increases, religion decreases. The secular stands in contrast to the religious setting of earlier societies where religion was everywhere, interwoven with everything else, and in no sense construed as a separate sphere of its own. The shift to secularity involves a move

---

[8]Charles Taylor, *The Secular Age* (Cambridge, MA: The Belknap Press of Harvard University Press, 2007), 9.
[9]See: Judith A. Merkle, *Discipleship, Secularity, and the Modern Self: Dancing to Silent Music* (London: Bloomsbury/T&T Clark, 2020).

from a society in which belief in God is unchallenged and, in most cases, unproblematic to one in which it is considered as one option among others—and not the easiest option to follow. Both believer and unbeliever live in this same context. Therefore, we have moved in our conditions of belief from a situation in which it was virtually impossible not to believe in God, to one in which faith, even for a strong believer, is one human possibility among others.[10]

While Taylor's initial descriptions of the secular climate might not fit all people in all circumstances, he offers a language to identify trends in culture which were not predominant in times past. Previously, they may have represented some elements of a culture, however, today they are more pervasive. Together they form a type of social imaginary, or how people unconsciously view their lives and their future. It can be argued that they also impact the culture within religious life itself.

A Different Way of Thinking

A common perception of the secular world is that it is simply the world of traditional values, the world we know, minus God. But, for Charles Taylor, it is not that simple: the secular world is an entirely different world.[11] The question is not whether the world is more or less religious, or whether we are living in an age of belief or an age of reason: Taylor is concerned with the conditions of belief, or what is believable today. What plausibility structures support religion and what ones contest it? While the prior contest faced by Christianity was between paganism and the axial religions, today exclusive humanism has become a radical new option. This reality has consequences for religious life today.

---

[10]Those from countries in the global south might find this description of secularity not appropriate for their context. It might need to be mixed with the multiple cultural factors which also impact the conditions of belief. However, members of these communities have remarked that as their societies modernize, and people move from agricultural settings to cities, things are changing. The conditions mentioned by Taylor do mark life in their larger cities and they can see these conditions as becoming more characteristic of those areas. This impact on their congregations needs to be acknowledged.

[11]Taylor, *A Secular Age*, 2–3.

Exclusive humanism is a type of option not offered in the same way to people in past centuries. Since the eighteenth century it has become possible to imagine a fulfilled human life without religion, and a sense of completion or fullness within the boundaries of a type of human perfection which can be reached in the "natural" passage from birth to death. We need not go beyond the boundaries of this life to reach fulfillment, nor do we need the love of God which takes us beyond human perfection through its power. There is no higher good. Taylor argues that the various reasons given for moderns "falling away" from religion are inadequate. Rather, modern identity as secular arises from new inventions, newly constructed self-understandings and practice, and cannot be explained in terms of perennial features of human life.

Modern Identity

Modern identity, or what it means to be human in secular society, is marked by a sense of inwardness, freedom, individuality, and being embedded in nature.[12] Moderns are aware of a sense of "self" as their center. Their sense of freedom and individuality is focused on the ordinary life and rejection of most hierarchies from earlier historical periods. Their sense of nature goes beyond an awareness of biological life; people also turn to nature as an inner moral source. Moderns are not without morals. Their aspirations of freedom, benevolence, and the affirmation of the ordinary life evoke a demand for universal justice, equality, self-rule, and beneficence that carry a sense of moral obligation which is almost unprecedented in human history. They put a high priority on ending suffering in society. While most agree on these standards, there is less agreement on the moral sources which underpin them. The pluralism of thought, as well as contradictions within schools of thought, become a source of cross pressures in modern life where the standards that are demanded of the modern person lack a conceptual support which can bear their requirements. For instance, helping the poor is important, but what grounds its continued practice over the long term when other choices conflict with it?

---

[12]Merkle, *Discipleship, Secularity and the Modern Self*, 35ff.

The modern person faces a dilemma as they encounter the tensions between the ideals of modern living on a principled level and its markers of success and fulfillment. Moderns are caught between two worlds. The nineteenth-century psychologist William James named this modern experience as an external one—the feeling of winds pulling you now here, and now there.

The Great Chain of Being

Traditionally, the moral stretch required to work toward universal beneficence was upheld generally in the West through a transcendent vision of God's *agape*, God's universal love for all. Secular thinking today would not uniformly support this vision, nor find it necessary. Modern people live in what is called an immanent frame: life without a transcendent reality. Instead of the world of the premodern period, one connected to a world beyond this one, many moderns live in a world where this world is all there is. Again, this description might not fit all people encountered, but Taylor argues it is significant enough to be more than a minority experience. The premodern world can be thought of as an enchanted one and the situation of modernity as one of disenchantment. The enchanted world was filled with spirits and moral forces, ones which impinge on human beings.[13] The boundary between the self and these forces was porous. The person was vulnerable to forces beyond the self— note the gargoyles on a medieval cathedral to ward off evil spirits. Superstition associated these forces with "magic" while religion linked them to the transcendent. An enchanted world turned to the cosmos for meaning, while a disenchanted one turns to self.

A more formal depiction of this world in premodern times was that of the world composed of a Great Chain of Being. One could understand how the world worked through understanding that being itself exists on several levels. The cosmos manifests a hierarchy and order. This hierarchy provides a key to understanding the real. The same superiority, for example, of the soul over the

---

[13]Charles Taylor, "Disenchantment – Reenchantment," in *Dilemmas and Connections: Selected Essays* (Cambridge, MA: The Belknap Press of Harvard University, 2011), 287–302.

body, the king over subjects, and the lion over the animal Kingdom "correspond" to order in other realms. The whole is bound together by realms of hierarchical complementarity. In the religious realm, there are objects in the enchanted world like the Host, or blessed candles, which deserve respect, not because I think so, but because they do.[14] The cosmos draws attention beyond itself and functions as a sign of what is more than nature. It testifies to the divine purpose and action. Its order and design point to the creator, and order and purpose for all created.[15] What things mean is independent of human perception or attribution. Individual actions have meaning in light of the order which unites human action, community, and the cosmos. This framework offers a vision of what is higher and lower, more important from less important, distinguishing the honorable from the less worthy.

What Works

In modern times, a "buffered self" replaces the porous self of days ago, and a new type of thought grows in importance. A reason that identifies problems and works toward their solution, or instrumental reason, feeds a different view of the world. The experience of modern life becomes possible. Focus shifts from attention to the purpose of life and the ends of our actions by an order beyond us, to the belief that human meanings are simply projected, arbitrarily conferred by humans. No other world of meaning gives significance to the present. Meaning rests in the "mind" not in reality outside the individual. For moderns, the only locus of thoughts, feelings, and spiritual energy or enthusiasm is in the mind. The only minds in the cosmos are human. The meaning or significance found in things rests not in them, but in the individual mind. Taylor claims that the difference between the mind-centered view and the enchanted world is that meanings are now "in the mind" and things only have meaning if they awaken a certain response in us.[16] In an enchanted world the person is porous to meanings outside the self. In a disenchanted world

---

[14]Taylor, *The Secular Age*, 161.
[15]Ibid., 25.
[16]Many have heard the teen response, "I'm not feeling it. I'm not into it."

the person is buffered from them. In the modern world, meaning comes into the world as it impinges on us and we react and give it meaning. The person is no longer vulnerable to the transcendent or the demonic. Humans live in a self-sufficient immanent order with a buffered identity. This is the world of disenchantment.[17]

This "turn" to the individual, who gives themselves meaning rather than receive from a broader order, opens the door to disengagement from cosmos and God. This makes exclusive humanism possible. In addition, it becomes possible to imagine meaning and significance within the universe itself, as an autonomous, independent meaning that is detached from any sort of transcendent dependence. Finally, disbelief no longer has social consequence since communal identity and welfare no longer rests on maintaining relationship with God. God does not give meaning to life nor ensures the victory of good over evil. Lack of orthodoxy no longer threatens the commonweal.[18] The energy of disenchantment is both positive and negative, according to Taylor. Its negative effect is that it mistook all spiritually charged realities as magic, thus people lost their capacity to distinguish between the truly spiritually symbolic and the magical. They also lost a language for it. At the same time, with the world pruned of the sacred and its limits, people could rationalize the world, expel mystery from it, yet re-order it as they saw fit. Taylor remarks, "A great energy is released to re-order affairs in secular time."[19] Religious grapple with this secular world, acknowledging their responsibility for the shape of society, yet also desiring to establish their religious identity in this climate.

A New Compass

Modernity brought an emergence of increasing interest in nature for its own sake, not simply as a manifestation of God, but as a concern manifested in science, art, and ethics. Since, in a modern mindset, the purposes things serve are extrinsic, not intrinsic to them, "changing" nature became easier. The Enlightenment belief that humans were to

---

[17]See: Judith A. Merkle, *Beyond Our Lights and Shadows: Charism and Institution in the Church* (London: Bloomsbury/T&T Clark, 2016), 88–9.
[18]Taylor, *The Secular Age*, 41–54.
[19]Ibid., 80.

dominate over nature and use nature for their purposes stemmed from this manner of thinking. Awareness that normative sensibilities still were needed to guide human initiative was eclipsed by a focus on what works.[20] Some looked to a "deep nature" for insights into an ethical direction, but not to a nature linked to the transcendent. In this secular mentality nature itself stands as a reservoir of good, of innocent desire or benevolence, and love of the good.

In the political realm, civil religion, rooted in a "natural" religion, was preferred as it could transcend denominational conflicts. It provided a spiritual identity not attached to a practicing community. The common project of pursuing a modern moral order became one of seeking mutual benefit.[21] The goal was a "polite society"—a type of self-sufficient image of living together in a society which has a civilizational goal that does not need the transcendent. People can set their own standards. The only transcendent references allowed are those which underpin the order already decided, do not infringe on it, or call for a higher standard, check aggressions, or limit economic choices.[22] What is acceptable or not acceptable is the rule. The modern moral order of mutual benefit enables those who live in it a disenchanted world where one can still experience moral fullness, without reference to God, within the range of purely intra-human powers.[23] The transcendent may not be totally absent, but it has certainly shrunk. Humans can make the world work without what has been known as grace. Christian love and the challenge of Christian universalism morphed into the affirmation of immanent resources for fullness and meaning. In Taylor's analysis, this forms the charter of modern unbelief.

The Role of Emotions

The Romantics protested a disengaged instrumental reason. They saw dangers in an absence of feeling, and their critique opened the

---

[20]Ibid., 98.
[21]Ibid., 237. See Also: James K. A. Smith, *How (Not) to Be Secular* (Grand Rapids, MI: Eerdmans, 2014), 53–4.
[22]Taylor, *A Secular Age*, 238–9.
[23]Ibid., 244–5.

door to new modern sensibilities. Romantics focused on the pursuit of pleasure and avoidance of pain, as well as the promotion of conditions where everyone defines his or her purposes in individual terms. Trust in one's own inner impulses leads one to the good in nature within oneself, they affirmed. To know what this is, men and women need to articulate what these impulses impel them to do. This led to new expressivism, fueled by sentiment.

However, critics charged that if the good life is described by sentiment, or feelings, departure from traditional moral codes is close at hand. The vibrancy to life provided by sensuality can offset the significance given to values like benevolence and solidarity in traditional settings. As people gave shape to what is within themselves through expressing it, the path to a new aliveness believed to be in their own nature also became the basis for a new and fuller individualism. Since each person is different and original, that originality, not traditional values, determines how he or she ought to live. Some of these shifts in the culture affected religious life itself.

Postmodern

The postmodern period offers a different turn to interiority than previous ones. The turn to experience was no longer understood as contact with the alignment of nature and reason, or instinct and creative power. The postmodern impulse is to a new unity, a new way of being. The key to this movement is to be open to a flux which moves beyond the scope of control or integration. The postmodern calls for a re-ordering of an unfamiliar kind. The center of gravity in the midst of flux appears as an "epiphany." It is displaced from the "self" in new forms of unity amid the flow of experience, even to new language—forming a type of structure.

In contrast to the ancients, who found what is deep and timeless in a world of external forms, moderns find this is an inwardness of experience, which, if one goes deep enough, will lead to an encounter with the mythic, the archetypical, and the luminous. What has changed since the era of the Great Chain of Being is that the Whole is indexed to a personal vision. There is an interweaving of the subjective and the transcendent.

These shifts in modernity make it more difficult to retrieve a sense of the Whole, as the pluralism of personal visions appears to leave a center lacking. A sense of the whole cannot be retrieved through ideas alone or returning to a premodern way of thought, even though some modern religious efforts attempt this. The Whole is the object of the search for fullness; Christian belief holds there is a link between the Spirit of God in the universe and the Spirit of God, as wholeness within the heart of believers. The movement toward the "more," which humans never fully reach, is also a movement toward the Whole, one that goes beyond the complete, perfect, or any end state that would contradict the nature of human existence as conflict-ridden, always becoming and contingent. Rather it is a movement toward what is, in the apophatic spiritual tradition, unknowable and ungraspable yet at the same time existentially foundational.

The Spirit of God is the one who creates the union between human beings and the mystery of God at the heart of everyday life. The whole of Life is the unfolding seed of the Reign of God and is expressed most clearly in the person of Jesus Christ. The paschal mystery of Jesus is not only the self-emptying of Jesus in love in his ministry and cross, and his glorification by the Father in the resurrection, but the giving of a share of his Spirit to all who believe (I Cor. 6:11, 12:13). The Spirit of God is the one who carries out the divine work of God's saving love for the world, established in Christ, to its completion.[24] The Spirit creates our union with God, with each other, and brings about the unity of all humankind (LG 1). When we seek to "sense the Spirit" we surrender to this Wholeness, never fully achieved, but only touched by surrender in faith.

For this reason, Christian beliefs are much more than facts; rather they are the transcendent data on which we rely to act. As truths of living, they cannot be detached from those who carry them into society by expressing them with their lives. It is the Body of Christ, fed by the Eucharist, who lives the gospel and carries its meaning in the modern world. What summons religious life today is the challenge of doing its part to embody the gospel in new times. Christians, through solidarity and creative imagination, are to express the reality of the love of God, shown most clearly in the

---

[24]John R. Sachs, S.J., "Holy Spirit in Christian Worship," in *The New Dictionary of Sacramental Worship*, ed. Peter E. Fink, S.J. (Collegeville, MN: The Liturgical Press, 1990), 529–39, at 535.

paschal mystery of Jesus, with their lives.[25] The first witness of the lives of religious, therefore, is not only the service they provide but their efforts to be authentic signs of this wholeness, of what life is about, in society today.

The Reign of God and Charism

Certainly, the identity of religious life is tied inseparably to the meaning of the Reign/Kingdom of God at a theological level. The Reign of God is the redemptive presence of God in our lives. Whenever we love each other, can forgive or bear with each other, work to build peace, and establish justice in our societies and serve our neighbor, the "rule" of God or how God wants things, is made evident. God's rule is the rule of love.[26] The Reign of God is liberating as it makes a difference in daily life. When Jesus described God's Kingdom/Reign in the Beatitudes (Mt. 5:1-11), he said access to it came to the poor in spirit, the persecuted, the meek, and the pure of heart. Those who will ultimately enter the Kingdom/Reign of God in heaven are those who respond to the needs of the poor (Mt. 25:31-46). God's presence at work manifests itself when the challenges of real life arise. We know God's Reign is the reality of God's life when, in our hearts, in groups, in institutions, and in creation itself, it creates, renews, and transforms.[27]

Just as there is no limit to the boundaries of the Reign of God, there is no limit to its time; it does not expire and is not static. The Kingdom/Reign is not just for the future; it is not to be identified only with heaven. As Christians pray the Our Father, "Thy Kingdom Come" they pray for God to come into life now in the present. At the same time, God has been there since the beginning, breathing life and movement into the world, present to creation itself—as Pope Francis reminds us in *Laudato Si'*.[28] The Reign of God broke in upon us in

---

[25]Merkle, *Discipleship, Secularity and the Modern Self*, 54.

[26]Karl Rahner, "Reflections on the Unity of the Love of Neighbor and the Love of God," in *Theological Investigations*, Vol. VI (New York: Crossroad, 1982).

[27]For a link between the beatitudes and a new asceticism in secular society see: Merkle, *Discipleship, Secularity and the Modern Self*, 159–75.

[28]See: Elizabeth T. Groppe, "The Love that Moves the Sun and Stars," in *The Theological and Ecological Vision of Laudato Si'*, ed. Vincent J. Miller (London: Bloomsbury/T&T Clark, 2017), 77–94.

a decisive way in the coming of Jesus Christ. In Christ's words, his ministry and works, and in his presence, the Reign of God reveals itself to us. The Kingdom/Reign is clearly visible in the very person of Christ, Son of God, who came to serve and give his life as a ransom for the many (LG 5). The life, death, and resurrection of Jesus Christ enabled the sending of the Spirit on to the apostles, and consequently on to all who believe the church and accept the mission to proclaim and establish the Kingdom among all peoples (GS 45). The mission of the church is to announce the Reign of God, which has already come through the sacraments, and its preaching. It is called to work with people of goodwill to bring about the Kingdom/Reign in the present through justice, peace, and reconciliation; and to be in its presence in the world a sacrament of the unity God intends with all humankind (LG 1). Finally, the church is called to point to the promise of fullness of life which comes with union with God both now and in the next life (Rev. 21:4-5). The church is not the Kingdom/Reign of God but is called to be a servant of humanity and witness to the continuing unfolding of the Kingdom/Reign in time.

The church is not equal to the Kingdom. It is one thing to insist that the church is the servant or instrument of the Reign of God. It is another matter entirely to suggest that the church is itself the Kingdom of God. Before Vatican II many Catholics said precisely that. We automatically assumed that whenever the New Testament speaks of the Kingdom of God, as in the many parables of the Kingdom, the New Testament was flatly identifying it with the church. Actually, it was not. The Reign of God is larger than the church. The gospel testifies, "Not everyone who says to me, 'Lord, Lord,' shall enter the Kingdom of heaven, but he who does the will of my Father who is in heaven will enter" (Mt. 7:21). It is common in the experience of the modern church to recognize the goodwill of those in our families, neighborhoods, and cities, yet who do not belong to the church. Their witness reinforces the words of St. Augustine as adapted by Karl Rahner, S.J., "Many whom God has, the Church does not have. And many whom the Church has, God does not have."[29]

---

[29]As quoted by Richard B. McBrien, "What is the Kingdom of God?" http://www.lovingjustwise.com. AmericanCatholic.org. Website from the Franciscans and St. Anthony Messenger.

This insight into the meaning of the Reign of God draws attention to two challenges facing the renewal of religious congregations today. There has been a great loss of authority and credibility on the part of the church because of the sexual abuse crisis. In former times, religious were identified as vanguards of the church. Some within religious congregations share the pain of the crisis along with the People of God. Identification with the church can be a negative element of life today. As a religious experiences this struggle and change of climate in the church, the paralysis of vision and spirit enters their own lives and ministry. Some envision the future of their congregations without the church, simply as a service organization with a broad religious focus, or without one. Many would argue this is not a positive direction for the future of religious life. Religious question the significance of the church as they live and work side-by-side with people of other faiths or no faith—but who share the ideals of their ministry in hospitals, schools, social work, and the like. The shift from a ministry style where religious were seen as the vanguard of the church, the "first responders" in ecclesial ministry, to an engagement in secular society challenges religious to claim their ecclesial identity in meaningful ways without denying their experience of the integrity of the lives of those with whom they minister and serve.

Charism and the Reign of God

At Vatican II the term "charism" was used fourteen times in the council documents, yet we find that the term is very difficult to pin down. The meaning of charism has been open to evolution in the life of the church as its reality as known today is not totally captured in scripture.[30] Yet its full identity in scripture and tradition is inseparable from its meaning for religious today.

The roots of a modern-day experience of charism are present in the scriptures since the early times of the faith community, through its reference to the Spirit. The Hebrew word *ruah*, in Greek *pneuma*,

---

[30]Albert Vanhoye, S.J., "The Biblical Question of '*Charisms*' after Vatican II," in *Vatican II: Assessment and Perspectives: Twenty-Five Years After (1962–1987)*, Vol. 1, ed. Rene Latourelle (Mahwah, NJ: Paulist Press, 1988), 439–68, esp. 440.

means breath, air, wind, or soul. While breath can mean the sign and principle of life, it has a less admirable sense, as "windy words," something unsubstantial (Job 16:3; Job 6:26). In the positive form it refers to the Spirit of God, that which comes from another dimension of reality. In the Hebrew scriptures, *ruah* denotes the wind or breath of air which is the force that enlivens human beings. Breath in this sense is a principle of human life; it is the ground of knowledge and feeling. It also indicates the life of God, the force by which God acts and causes action.[31] Breath is not the same as flesh, the term used in the scriptures to refer to the earthly reality of human life. Flesh is weak and corruptible, whereas spirit breath is the life principle. This breath, or Spirit, connects our life to God, our meaning to God's meaning. The spirit breath is first and foremost what causes human beings to act, so that God's plan, or reign, in history may be fulfilled.[32]

The spirit, or breath, in the Hebrew scripture has an effect on human beings, as it brings about an experience of seeing and wisdom. The guidance and inspiration given by the Spirit are attributed to the breath of God himself. While the Spirit comes from God, it is not other-worldly. It gives discernment and wisdom that deals with what is normal. Through ordinary occurrences of life, human encounters with God guarantee that God's plan for his people will be carried out. The purposes of these encounters transcend the individual. They are meant as vehicles of God's continual movement toward God's people with all their needs and concerns, to the point of even animating their dead bones (Ezek. 36-38). God will do this by communicating himself within people's hearts. "A new heart I will give you, and a new spirit I will put within you; and I will remove from your body the heart of stone and give you a heart of flesh. I will put my spirit within you, and make you follow my statues and be careful to observe my ordinances." (Ezek. 36:26-28) The judges and the prophets in the Hebrew scripture were seen as means through which God moved toward his people and cared for them.

---

[31]John L. McKenzie, S.J., *The Dictionary of the Bible* (Milwaukee, WI: The Bruce Publishing Co., 1966), 840.
[32]Yves Congar, O.P., *I Believe in the Holy Spirit. The Complete Three Volume Work in One Volume*, trans. David Smith (New York: Crossroad, 1983), 3-15.

When early Christians made their confession of faith, their belief in the Holy Spirit was linked to the one "who had spoken through the prophets." The Spirit by whom Jesus was conceived, who animated the gospel, was the same Spirit referred to in the Hebrew scripture.[33] In the New Testament the most important elements in the experience and revelation of this Spirit are the conception, baptism, and activity of Jesus. Luke shows in the Acts of the Apostles that the Spirit which anointed Jesus at Nazareth, and especially at his baptism in the Jordan, was also sent to the church. Pentecost was for the church what his baptism was for Jesus: the gift and the power of the Spirit, dedication to the ministry, mission, and bearing witness.[34] The New Testament refers both to the Spirit and to God's favor or *charis*. In fact, the whole message of the Gospel as Good News is captured in the term God's favor to us. In particular, and most frequently, *charis* means the saving will of God executed in Jesus Christ and communicated to men and women through him. Jesus is both the object and the expression of the goodwill of God. Hence in the New Testament *charis* means both favor, an act immanent to God, and the effects of the saving will as they appear in the life of Jesus and in the church.[35]

St. Paul

St. Paul's experience in the beginning of the church leads him to use the word "charism" to capture its unfolding. Charism refers to the gift of grace: importantly the gift of redemption and eternal life (Rom. 5:15-16, 6:23). Yet he also uses it to refer to particular gifts like those given to the people of Israel (Rom. 11:29); grace given to ministers of evangelization (1 Cor. 12:8-10, 29-30, Rom. 12:6-8); as well as the gift of bodily healings (1 Cor. 12:30). *Charis* refers to the graces that establish a person in a way of life in the church— virginity, marriage, and pastoral ministry—conferred by the laying on of hands (1 Cor. 7:7, cf. 1 Tim. 4:14, 2 Tim. 1:6).

---

[33]Ibid.
[34]Ibid., 19, also 15–24.
[35]McKenzie, *The Dictionary of the Bible*, 324.

Paul's approach is characterized by the effort shown in 1 Corinthians 12-14 to distinguish charism from what was experienced in the early church as mere "enthusiasm" and strange ecstatic phenomena. He focuses rather on the place of charism in the ordered life of the community; instead of seeing charisms as belonging only to the specialized few, he sees them as characteristic of the baptized in general (Rom. 12:6; 1 Cor. 7:7).[36]

Paul uses the metaphor of the body and its members to show that the variety of the gifts of the Spirit is not contrary to the unity of the church—rather it is necessary to it. Charisms, as grace, are given to build up the Body of Christ. Paul lists the charisms: he names apostles first, then prophets, and others after them (1 Cor. 1:4-7; 12:4-11). Key to understanding Paul's assessment of the charismatic gifts is that they are all subordinate to the main gift of the Christian life, the gift of love (1 Cor. 13). And, unlike the charisms which are transient, love will not pass away.[37] No one has all the charisms, nor needs them. In fact charisms are the principle differentiation in the Body of Christ (1 Cor. 12:4-11). Some have argued that charismata were only phenomena at the beginning of the church, and that the further institutional developments of the church were deviations from its primitive beginnings.[38] However, Walter Kasper argues that we need to read the New Testament accounts of the charismata in the context of the accounts of Jesus' miracles and the miracles of the apostles (Mt. 6:7; 16:17-18, 20; Acts 2:2, 43; 4:3; 5:12ff; Heb. 2:4). In this deeper context the charismata are signs of the beginning of the Kingdom of God and therefore they belong permanently to the church.[39] In fact, after the council, the rediscovery of the charismatic dimension of the church became the basis of various renewal movements. The council also recognized the activity of the Spirit outside the visible Catholic Church (LG 15, UR 3).

Understanding the renewal of religious life as an unfolding seed and the search of religious as "sensing the Spirit" is enriched by

---

[36]Estevao Bettencourt, "Charism," in *Sacramentum Mundi*, Vol. 1, ed. Karl Rahner et al. (New York: Herder and Herder, 1968), 283–4 at 283.
[37]Wilfred Harrington, O.P., "Charism," in *The New Dictionary of Theology*, ed. Joseph A. Komonchak et al. (Wilmington, DL: Michael Glazier, 1989), 180–3.
[38]Walter Kasper, *The Catholic Church: Nature, Reality and Mission* (London: Bloomsbury, 2015), 189.
[39]Ibid., 138.

recognizing we cannot draw up an exhaustive list of charisms in the New Testament. To do so would assume the Spirit is limited to giving only those gifts to the church now, which he had already given to the church at apostolic times. Certainly the Holy Spirit, who guides the church through times, will continue to give new gifts to meet new needs in every age. Yves Congar provides perspective on this more general statement, to mean that the Spirit (at Pentecost) did not come simply to animate an institution that was already fully determined in all its structures, but that he is really the "co-instituting principle."[40]

Charism Today

Before Vatican II, charism was usually related to extraordinary gifts of the Spirit, not to the ordinary life of the Christian. However, today, understanding the charism of religious life must be integrated into a wider acknowledgment of its presence in the church. Religious also have a role in recognizing the charisms of the laity and facilitating their incorporation into the life of the church. The council called for this inclusion but did not create structures for it to happen.[41] While in the encyclical *Mystici Corporis* Pius XII named charisms as marvelous gifts in the church, they were still viewed as rare and marginal phenomena. Vatican II saw charism given to the "faithful of every order." The church is called to gather and appreciate the many forms of grace given by God—charisms here are functional gifts that render the faith of every rank "fitted and made ready to assume various works and offices for the good of the church" (LG 12). This calls all members of the church to work toward what is necessary to integrate a renewed interest in charism with the institution of the church as a whole—a call which involves a growth both in spirituality and in structural reform. Today the charism of a congregation plays a key part in this process. Through the response of individuals and communities to the charism of founders and

---

[40]Congar, *I Believe in the Holy Spirit*, "He is the Lord and Giver of Life," Vol. II, 9.
[41]Ibid., 38–9, 126, 131–2, 195–7. Canonically, religious themselves are part of the laity.

foundresses they follow in new times the trajectory of grace it expresses, while adding their own response to its significance.

Karl Rahner reinforces why the charism in a religious congregation is important. God assures the victory of grace in our lives, in the history of society, and in the church as a whole, ordinarily through the institutions—not simply through the efforts of individuals alone. Human freedom is weak and defective. However, through God's action in a charism, a person is enabled to be faithful in freedom to living within a framework of life.[42] Our modern lens on living can be clouded by a sole focus on the individual. Understanding this wider view focuses on life beyond what we can imagine and accomplish alone. Charism in this sense is integral to the process of the renewal of religious life today. As an unfolding seed already in our midst, this renewal cannot be enacted in isolation from others in community and the rest of the church and society.

Shifts in Understanding the Christian Life

The meaning of religious life has always involved witness to Jesus Christ, service to the church, desire to bring about the Kingdom, and intention to follow a path to God. Religious life has as its ultimate goal love of God and neighbor. However, religious life has also been interpreted in terms of general understandings of the Christian life in the period in which it existed. Before Vatican II it was not uncommon for religious life to be understood with emphasis on rule-keeping, avoidance of obstacles to a spiritual life, and focus on behaviors of order or custom as measures of fidelity. The vows of poverty, celibate chastity, and obedience were also interpreted within this paradigm. They were presented as a means for overcoming attachment to possessions, sexual pleasure, power, and pride. Beyond the commandments, the vows were an additional set of obligations and ascetical practices which expressed a life dedicated to God. Some explain the vowed life as a type of "virtue ethics." The vows, in this approach, were viewed in light of the role they had in forming the type of person one becomes by living them; more than an assessment of right and wrong behaviors attached to

---

[42]Karl Rahner, "The Certainty of Faith," in *The Practice of Faith* (New York: Crossroad, 1983), 32ff.

them. The language of perfection encompasses both explanations. The first approach focuses on removing obstacles to perfection; the second emphasizes developing the habits of perfection. The language of perfection in both accounts relies on a style of clear behaviors as measures of faithfulness. "Keep the rule and the rule will keep you," is the advice given. Most religious worked through the limitations of this framework through integration of broader spiritual insights into their lives and spirituality.

Frameworks for Understanding Christian Living

How we understood religious life before Vatican II flowed from a general conception of the moral life in Catholicism. The major paradigm for understanding moral responsibility was the scholastic view of the human person. It focuses on the action of the individual and is compatible with the need for a confessor in the Sacrament of Penance to assess moral culpability. This approach to morality understands the person as someone who thinks and makes choices. Sin is a deliberate act against the law of reason, which is inherent to one's own rational nature. Moral evil is created through free will: the ability to act or not to act, and to act in one way or another. Attention to individual responsibility and assessment of personal freedom remains the first language of moral theology in the church. It concurs with the Vatican II affirmation that, within the foundations of conscience of all human beings, there are nonconventional, nonarbitrary moral standards which make possible genuine self-criticism and so true moral knowledge even for those who have not be exposed to the instruction of divine revelation. It is possible to know right from wrong and to make a free choice. This affirms that there are moral standards which are not simply the results of personal preference or choice or of social conventions.[43]

Vatican II enriched this understanding of the Christian life with a deeper theology of the Christian life. It offered a renewed emphasis

---

[43]Joseph Boyle, "Natural Law," in *The New Dictionary of Theology*, ed. Joseph A. Komonchak, Mary Collins and Dermot A. Lane (Collegeville, MN: Liturgical Press, 1987), 703–8.

on following Jesus Christ and a sense of social responsibility as integral to the meaning of faithfulness. The heart of Christian morality is the following of Jesus Christ. The council affirmed that a signature of Christian fidelity is acceptance of the salvation God offers us in and through Jesus Christ.[44] This acceptance in faith is made concrete by living by the example of Jesus. The call in the gift of salvation is to bring about a change in one's perception of reality and values, not just once, but throughout one's life. It is an invitation to ongoing conversion. Our effort to live a moral life is a response to this gift. The call of one's baptism is to live the Christian life not "in general" but in a particular context. Christians understand moral responsibilities given to all in a way peculiar to their situations and context. They also practice virtues and act in solidarity according to the realities in which they are embedded.[45]

How do these developments in Christian morality, called for by Vatican II, affect an understanding of religious life? The call to faithfulness of the gospel is more than one of personal moral rectitude understood as keeping moral codes or avoiding sin. Christians in this world are to allow their Christian faith to animate and direct the situation to which they are inserted. They are to do all they can to transform their culture and direct it to serve the common good. Christian faithfulness is more than following the gospel as if it offers a clear ethical blueprint of what to do or not to do. The call of one's baptism is not only one to avoid sin, but also to live constructively with and for others. Christians carry out these calls through the light and power of God's grace operating in the conditions of their life. However, this light does not replace their responsibility for this world to be active for the good, to use their reason, skills, and best information to make decisions for human betterment. Religious life in this understanding is not a "flight from the world" but an engagement in it.

These shifts in the general understanding of the moral life since Vatican II frame religious life with the same challenges and

---

[44]John Paul II, *Sources of Renewal: The Implementation of the Second Vatican Council* (London: Collins, 1980), 87.
[45]Peter Schnieller, *A Handbook of Inculturation* (New York: Paulist, 1990), 1. See also: Judith A. Merkle, *Being Faithful: Moral Commitment in Modern Society* (London: Bloomsbury/T&T Clark, 2010), chapter one.

necessary encounters embraced by the whole church. Christian faithfulness, in imitation of Jesus Christ, will always assume an incarnational bias. It aims at ". . . the intimate transformation of authentic human values through their integration in Christianity in the various human cultures." (RM 52.2) It is at core faithfulness in this world and responsibility for the shape of the world. For this reason the role of context in the moral life, and in an understanding of religious life today, has increasing importance.

Context and Religious Life

When moral theology in the church was focused mainly on the confessional, intention and circumstances were simply details in assessing accountability for a specific behavior. Today an expanded understanding of context involves its consideration through attention to the personal, social, and cultural realities it brings to a person's life. Personal context includes personal history, character, aptitude, and one's story. Social context refers to transpersonal realities which impact moral experience; for instance, one's place or power in a social situation, issues of race, class, gender, generation, and the impact of institutional arrangements on one's range of choice in life and ministry. Cultural contexts involve the assumptions that are the unnoticed and pre-reflective lenses through which people view life and their relationships. To some degree, we are aware of these complexities as we live day by day. However, context has a role as religious assess a new member, the goals of a regional community, or the priorities of a minority group in the congregation.

To leave context and culture and its impact out of our understanding of a faithful life and of religious life is to fail to be serious about the project of following Jesus Christ in the real world in which we live, and by people with modern goals and sensibilities.[46] While any of the three dimensions can enlarge, limit,

---

[46]See: Laurie Brink, *The Heavens Are Telling the Glory of God: An Emerging Chapter for Religious Life. Science, Theology and Mission* (Collegeville, MN: Liturgical Press, 2022). Here the author engages in a thought experiment on generational differences in religious life especially those around new science.

or shift moral responsibility and moral possibilities in a situation, they also contextualize the path of personal integration, social immersion, ecclesial service, and, for religious, the understanding and living of the vows.[47] As new members consider religious life, how congregations understand these elements of their common life influences whether their doors are really open to new life and possibilities. For religious today, being faithful still shares a universal identity but context also situates and affects its expression. Often this diversity of contexts raises more questions than answers as we move into the future.[48] As we continue to sense where the Spirit may be leading as we engage in the unfolding of religious life, these issues will be interwoven in our concerns.

---

[47]Merkle, *Being Faithful*, 173–86. See also: 7–18.

[48]This text explores interculturality in religious life. *Engaging Our Diversity: Interculturality and Consecrated Life Today*, ed. Maria Cimperman, RSCJ, and Roger P. Schroeder, SVD (Maryknoll, NY: Orbis Books, 2020). See also: Mary Johnson, SNDdeN, Mary Gautier and Patricia Wittberg SC, Do, Thu, LHC. *Migration for Mission: International Catholic Sisters in the United States* (New York: Oxford University Press, 2019).

2

The Niche of Religious Life

The concept of a niche is used in ecology and evolution. The niche is about the interrelationships between one species and its environment, including other species.[1] The image of a niche can prove to be useful in grasping the changed situation of religious life. While niche is an ecological concept, it also has evolutionary consequences. Changes in a niche can have implications on whether a species becomes extinct or evolves. Understanding the workings of a niche may render some insight as to how to move forward, as we consider the changes which have occurred in religious congregations since Vatican II.

The Niche

Science stipulates that two species cannot occupy the same niche. If two competing species coexist in a stable environment, they do so because of niche differentiation: each finds a place where it can thrive. Religious congregations since Vatican II certainly differ from their enclosed past. Secular society offers religious a different niche. Environmentalists claim that the fundamental niche of an organism contains all the requirements and conditions needed for survival. This may be different from its actual niche, or how it lives. In the actual niche there can be elements which constrain the organism. Competing species consume each other or the resources a species

---

[1]Terrence P. Ehrman, C.S.C. "Ecology: The Science of Interconnections," in *The Theological and Ecological Vision of Laudato Si'*, ed. Vincent J. Miller (London: Bloomsbury/T&T Clark, 2017), 58–61.

needs for its survival. Some species can so constrain the fundamental niche of another that its actual niche disappears, and the species goes locally or globally extinct.

These concepts may seem remote from the situation of religious life today yet, as a thought experiment, the idea of the niche can be an analogical tool to identify elements which influence religious congregations. A niche symbolizes many factors which impact congregations: religious, cultural, financial, actuarial, civil, and ecclesial. Scientists claim that if you disturb a niche, a species cannot live there. However, extinction is not the only option; a new species can be created. The niche of religious life has changed many times throughout history. The hope is that, by attention to these and recent changes, the conditions in which religious life grows may become more evident.

The Foundations of a Lifestyle

When St. Benedict (480–547) wrote his rule for monastic life, *Rule for Monasteries*, he intended it to be a Christian lifestyle that an ordinary person could follow. There was a shift in understanding that the shedding of blood was the main form of heroic virtue and witness to Christ after the age of the martyrs. Martyrdom was neither the only model of Christian witness nor a sole characteristic of a follower of Jesus or a disciple. Thought widened to include what Max Weber, the nineteenth-century sociologist, called a *virtuosi*. This is someone within a spiritual tradition who focuses on attaining, or helping others to attain, some form of inner spiritual perfection. Usually *virtuosi* separated from the world or were mendicants within it. Even many centuries before Christ, men and women of the great religions pursued the monastic life. They went to mountainous heights, caves, and deserts seeking, through a geographical apartness, a way to overcome the worldliness which interrupted their spiritual pursuit of closeness to God. They sought the wisdom and the tools others had outlined to master their own inner worldliness. The goal of monasticism was purity of heart, emptying the heart of earthly attachments, so that it could be free, be silent, hear God, and pray always.[2]

---

[2]Basil M. Pennington, OCSO, "Monasticism," in *The New Dictionary of Theology*, ed. Joseph A. Komonchak, Mary Collins, and Dermot Lane (Wilmington, DE: Michael Glazier, 1989), 670–3.

In the early years of the church, apartness did not require fleeing to the desert. Persecutions, exile, and death were frequent realities of the Christian life. As Christianity was incorporated into the broader society it also melded with it and took on its distractions. In response, people fled to find greater solitude, living on the edge of communities or in the desert to find separation from what was felt to be a world hostile to the values of the gospel. The disparities between Christian ideals and a cultural system increasingly based on materialistic progress became evident. Conflicts accounted in ancient texts reflect the clashes between gospel ideals and societal realities. Saint Basil the Great reports the agony of a poor father deciding which of his children he will select to sell into servitude in order to feed the rest of his family, as the "buyer" haggles for a lower and lower price.[3]

Early *virtuosi* found that the prevailing cultural values were not worth the investment of their lives. In response, typically their lives took two forms: they lived in the desert completely on their own, gathered around a holy man or woman; or they formed communities under the guidance of a superior. One finds these lifestyles in both the Eastern and Western church.

The monasticism which developed during the fourth and fifth centuries in the Mediterranean world was a development of these early attempts at an alternative way of living. It did so in a context where a few were affluent and many were enslaved. However, the wealthy, aristocratic, and socially prominent also became monks.[4] People left the lecture halls of Rome and Athens, government positions and successful enterprises, prosperous families, and great estates to look for wisdom greater than that offered by their culture. When St. Benedict wrote his rule, he drew from various monastic traditions, as monastic life was not uniform. He also addressed some of the excesses of drifting and indulgences which had arisen in monastic practice. Not all those who attempted to live religious life did so with excellence. Benedict wanted the structure he set to continually call them to fidelity.

---

[3]Daniel Finn, *Christian Economic Ethics* (Minneapolis, MN: Fortress Press, 2013).
[4]Peter Brown, *The Body and Society: Men, Women and Sexual Renunciation in Early Christianity* (New York: Columbia University Press, 1988), 410.

Benedict insisted on *obedience* to a superior to curb the will. For those who lived in small groups, obedience was necessary as, "their law is what they like to do . . . whatever strikes their fancy." He called for *stability* to counter drifting and wandering, noting that some monks never took the journey they intended to live—"they never settled down, and are slaves to their own wills and gross appetites." *Fidelity* to a rule was offered as a school of conversion, as living under a rule and an abbot brought about a discipline that one is likely not to impose on oneself.[5] A healthy liturgical life, labor, and time for reading to nourish prayer were to support monastic life and give it balance. Monastic life was not only to express a love of God but also to enkindle it, therefore its structure was important.

In the Middle Ages monastic life focused on the Rule as a *school of love*, and on community. Community life was to support the monk or nun and help them to learn to love God by loving and desiring to be loved by their monastic brethren. For medieval men and women, such as Claire and Francis of Assisi, one becomes one true self through conformity to the model of true humanity, Jesus Christ. By the Middle Ages the monastic life, while contemplative and ascetical in its roots, had an immense social, economic, and political impact on society. Both men and women found in their inner religious experience an energy to engage in political affairs, or challenge cultural norms in society and in the church: Francis of Assisi countered the opulence of the church; Catherine of Siena advised the pope; and armies were led by Joan of Arc. They witnessed the inseparability of religious and "worldly experience", which was to be a signature of *virtuosi* experience in the modern age. Monastic groups of the Middle Ages did perform social services: they ran monastic schools, and cared for the sick or aged, but they were not usually founded for this reason. Their main "work" was saving souls; the by-product of evangelization was other charitable practices.

The Reformation no longer saw monasticism as the special place to experience God; rather God was seen to be present intensely in all

---

[5]Pennington, "Monasticism," 672. See also, Judith A. Merkle, *Discipleship, Secularity and the Modern Self: Dancing to Silent Music* (London: Bloomsbury/T&T Clark, 2020), 130–2.

of life.[6] All men and women were called equally to holiness within their everyday lives; the idea of a separate and superior virtuoso state was not a focus. Catholics were impacted by the challenges of the Reformers and questioned the traditional spiritually-focused religious virtuosity practiced in the Middle Ages. Founders and Foundresses of new religious orders, however, combined active service-teaching, nursing, and caring for the poor with spiritual exercises. Ignatius of Loyola, Vincent de Paul, and Angela Merici, for example, pioneered a new form of religious virtuosity within Catholicism. Protestants, on the other hand, tended to see the state, the Christian commonwealth—not monastic *virtuosi*—as responsible to provide schools, hospitals, and social services for the poor, the sick, and the uneducated.

Patricia Wittberg, in her sociological study of modern religious life, claims that religious traditions that deny the value of a separate, inner-oriented form of religious virtuosity, as the Protestant reformers did, are relatively rare. For a religion to develop an alternative form of virtuosity focused on external service to the larger society, as did Catholicism after the Reformation, is also unusual. For several hundred years, however, a hybrid form of religiosity within Catholicism was essential to the social interventions of the wider mission of the church. The church wished to address the social dislocations of an industrializing Europe and North America. During the nineteenth century the number of new active orders grew enormously, and those orders who continued to follow the traditional, contemplative, version of Catholic virtuosity steadily declined.[7] The difference between the social works of these orders, and the good works of the monastic communities of previous centuries, was that the service dispensed was not by individuals on a one-to-one basis but through large-scale institutions maintained by members. In this new situation, *virtuosi* did not ordinarily live in monasteries, but among the people they served. These changes indicate major ways the *niche* of religious life was shaped dramatically by the needs of the mission of the church in the industrial age.

[6]Patricia Wittberg, *From Piety to Professionalism and Back: Transformations of Organized Religious Virtuosi* (Lanham, MD: Lexington Books, 2006), 5–6.
[7]Ibid., 6.

Virtuosi and the Industrial Age

A key pastoral strategy for the church to carry out its mission and support its members in a new industrial society was Catholic Action. The aims of this movement were to repair or reconstruct Christian civilization where it has been injured or destroyed through the forces of modernization. Its three strategies were: to disseminate a better knowledge of Catholic social principles and ideals as well as the Catholic faith itself; to reorganize the public life of individual nations in accordance with Catholic standards; and, lastly, to counteract the poverty, insecurity, and material misery of the laboring population.[8] A strategy of Catholic Action was the creation of parallel institutions within industrial society. Catholic hospitals, schools, newspapers, political parties, and the like were organized under the banner of "Catholic Action."[9] The *niche* of religious orders fell into this wider pastoral plan. More than 600 new religious orders were founded in Catholicism worldwide between 1800 and 1900, almost all of which were devoted to teaching, nursing, or social work.

Both Catholic and Protestant *virtuosi* took on new forms to meet the needs of industrial society. After the mid-nineteenth century the *niche* of religious life was changed through the way it dispensed service to others. The works of charity were no longer done primarily by individuals on a personalized basis, one-to-one or within convents or their homes as before, in the sixteenth century. Both Catholics and Protestants offered these services through large-scale institutions, sometimes in competition with one another. Catholic members of religious communities of men and women lived often in small groups among the people they served. A shared characteristic of both groups was that the active provision of needed services was given equal, if not greater, weight over prayer and personal spiritual growth.[10]

---

[8]Hubert Jedin, "Pope Benedict XV, Pius XI, and Pius XII," in *History of the Church in the Modern Age*, ed. Hubert Jedin (London: Burns and Oates, 1981), 26. See also: Edward Cahill, S.J. "The Catholic Movement: Historical Aspects," in *Readings in Moral Theology, No. 5 Official Catholic Social Teaching*, ed. Charles Curran (New York: Paulist Press, 1986), 5.
[9]Merkle, *Discipleship, Secularity and the Modern Self*, 129ff.
[10]Wittberg, *From Piety to Professionalism and Back*, 8–11. Home mission societies, Sunday schools, Deaconess houses, hospitals, orphanages, social work, Dorcas

Sponsoring Institutions

The relationships between these institutions and their sponsoring denominations varied. Forms of funding, staffing, and administration were done through a variety of formal and informal arrangements. In the Catholic Church, even though religious congregations functioned within the wider vision of the church's mission, the relationship between the church, the school, the hospital, the social service agency, and the state differed from country to country. Some congregations were international and functioned across national boundaries; others were local under a diocesan bishop. Through the twentieth into the twenty-first century these relationships continued to shift. Wittberg notes, "As their schools, hospitals and social service agencies grew, the role of the sponsoring group often changed from providing services themselves, to supervising others who provided them, and, finally to controlling, through their presence on the boards of directors, those who administered the provision of services."[11] The *niche* of religious congregations changed as these institutions expanded and professionalized. Those who began the institutions were increasingly outnumbered by officially credentialed lay professionals, as well as within congregations there was a higher standard set for the professional training of members. Institutions that had been owned by religious groups in some instances became incorporated under lay boards. Denominational hospitals or colleges merged with other public and nonprofit institutions, some of which had been previous competitors.

In the twenty-first century debates have ensued about whether these institutions can any longer be considered religiously distinctive.[12] Efforts toward placing "Mission Effectiveness" personnel in the administration are seen as an inadequate substitution for implementing the spirit of the sponsoring group. But, for our interests, the *niche* of the sponsoring congregations

---

societies for the relief of the poor, and foreign mission societies were among the organized efforts of men and women in the Protestant church,
[11]Ibid., 11.
[12]See: Charles Curran, *The Social Mission of the U.S. Catholic Church: A Theological Perspective* (Washington, DC: Georgetown University Press, 2010).

has also altered. Given that hospitals, sponsored schools, and social agencies have been changed by their absence, religious congregations themselves have experienced changes in key areas of their corporate life during this journey. The impact on recruitment of new members, changed relationships with the church at large, new expectations of leadership, and questions regarding the identity and culture of the congregation illustrate how the *niche* of religious life has been affected. [13]

A Change in Theology

The *niche* of religious life is also altered by the theology which sustains it. While the basis of religious life is rooted in the gospel and early monasticism, its shape in subsequent centuries also required an underlying theology and spirituality to ground it. We have seen that, while the Catholic Action movement framed the sense of mission of many religious congregations, the niche of their internal life was shaped also by canon law. Congregations do have a particular law that guides their unique group, but they also share broad outlines of their life through a common law affecting all congregations. By the 1950s religious life had become so unified through the Canon law code of 1917[14] that religious congregations were asked to study their "primitive spirit" or fundamental charism as a lens on renewal of their congregations for changing times.[15]

Even though every individual in the Christian life has a charism, groups have them as well. Charism in a religious community reflects a deep story of a community, often centred in the response and holiness of a founder or foundress. Over time this beginning became concretized in a *gestalt* of virtue to which a person can adhere, in a tradition or patterned "way," to God within the Christian life. Often a community's charism is also expressed in dedication to a particular work or set of works. While the church's mission as

---

[13]Wittberg, *From Piety to Professionalism and Back*, 12. This fact is the focus of Wittberg's important study.
[14]Judith Merkle, *A Different Touch: A Study of the Vows in Religious Life* (Collegeville, MN: The Liturgical Press, 1998), 129–30, 143ff.
[15]Maryanne Confoy, *Religious Life and Priesthood: Rediscovering Vatican II* (New York: Paulist, 2008), 178ff.

conceived in Catholic Action provided the ideology which sustained the works of apostolic congregations in institutional forms, it also impacted the identity of the congregation by defining characteristics of its self-identity.

Vatican II (1962–5) embraced a changed understanding of the church and its mission which shifted how communities and individuals understood their charism, eventually their mission, and in many cases their lifestyle. The Catholic Action model was gradually abridged by this new understanding, which held implications in congregations and the church. Issues from this change are far from resolved even today. Vatican II placed the theological and pastoral treatment of the church at the forefront: it emphasized the religious nature of the church. Instead of a primary self-identity as an institution, it stressed its religious nature through images of the church as the People of God, the Body of Christ, and the sacrament of salvation.

The shift at Vatican II from an institutional to a theological understanding of the church proved significant for defining the church's social mission and its impact on society.[16] When the church is seen in its religious nature and understood as a sacrament, rather than simply in its institutional structures as a hierarchical organization, its social mission is reinterpreted. There is a shift also in the meaning or ideological structure which supports its works. The social mission is no longer one of the tasks that the institution performs. Instead, the social mission is a symbol and sacrament of the religious nature of the church. The church expresses and symbolizes itself in doing its social mission. How the church, and subsequently congregations, engaged the society thus took on a new importance. The Synod of Bishops in 1971 claimed justice is a constitutive dimension of the church. "Action on behalf of justice and participation in the transformation of the world full appear to us as a constitutive dimension of the preaching of the Gospel, or, in other worlds, of the Church's mission for the redemption of the human race and its liberation from every oppressive situation" (JW 36).

---

[16]Francis Schussler Fiorenza, "Social Mission of the Church," in *The New Dictionary of Catholic Social Thought*, ed. Judith A. Dwyer (Collegeville, MN: The Liturgical Press, 1994), 151–71.

The Actual and Realized Niche

Many congregations, through their chapters and corporate decisions, began to implement this new understanding of mission. Maryanne Conroy concretizes the meaning of this shift in religious orders and the tensions which arose. An illustration of this change in understanding concerns the mission of the Christian Brothers, a religious order of men in the church. The Christian Brothers were initially established in Ireland with an international educational outreach. However, they moved from education in schools to establish a collaborative Edmund Rice International, a nongovernmental organization committed to advocacy on behalf of children and young people who are marginalized because of poverty, legal status, environmental degradation, or adult wars. It is sponsored by the Congregational of Christian Brothers and the Congregation of Presentation Brothers. It is a partner organization with Franciscan International in Geneva.[17] This change is symbolic of many congregations in the church who have diversified their ministries from what may have been their initial focus. The Brothers maintained many of their schools, but they also engaged in new endeavors. The change in the understanding of the mission of the church, which provided ideological grounding for their previous works, drew them to reinterpret their charism with a new expression.

Studies also show that the call to return to the spirit of their founder or foundress through a re-interpretation of works shifted the niche of congregations. If we remember, a fundamental niche, what it needs to survive, may be different from what exists in the actual niche, how it accommodates new organisms and circumstances. A fundamental niche can be so constrained by trying to integrate the niche of another, that its realized niche disappears, and the species goes extinct.

Studies done on religious congregations found that the absence of corporate commitment to embody the group's response to current un-met needs stood in contrast to the collective vision and action that marked the birth of most apostolic monastic or contemplative

---

[17]Confoy, *Religious Life and Priesthood*, 322 n.251.

congregations.[18] The type of communal culture present at the founding of the congregation no longer existed in modern society. Those in formation of new members questioned whether the communal formation of the past was the only possible model of community for religious life. New members asked where the communities who lived the community culture that was being taught were. The way the church imagined culture itself changed at Vatican II, as well as how the church and congregations interacted with the broader society.[19]

A Changed Understanding of Culture

A commonplace insight into religious life today is that the culture around it has changed. In the post-Second World War period, it was assumed that Catholic culture was a type of unified whole of beliefs simply transmitted to every Catholic. Catholics engaged in a common engagement in their societies around key values centered on human dignity.[20] A sense of a unified culture, linked to religion, was also mirrored in society. Stephen Carter claims that Americans look at the 1950s and early 1960s as the golden age of American society. Early TV programs mirrored a world where traditional values, order, and propriety set the stage for a non-conflictual social life built on a common agreement of general standards of living. Carter argues however that behind the public façade of this "golden age," those whose lives did not fit this image suffered.[21]

---

[18]David Nygren and Miriam Ukeritis, "Executive Summary of Study on the Future of Religious Orders," *Origins* 22/15, September 24, 1992, 270, as quoted in Confoy, *Religious Life and Priesthood*, 250.

[19]Michael Paul Gallagher S.J., *Clashing Symbols: An Introduction to Faith and Culture* (New York: Paulist Press, 2003).

[20]David O'Brien, "American Catholic and American Society," in *Catholics and Nuclear War*, ed. Philip J. Murnion (London: Geoffrey Chapman, 1983), 16–29.

[21]Stephen Carter, *Civility, Manners, Morals and the Etiquette of Democracy* (New York: Harper Collins, 1998). He notes that domestic abuse was transparent, patterns of bigotry and racism were accepted as "the ways things are," poverty was blamed on the victim, women were marginalized from public advancement, anyone not white and middle class was an outsider. The "good old days" were not as good as we thought.

Catholic theology prior to Vatican II imagined a split between the natural order and the supernatural. This theological understanding of the world depicted the world in terms of the church, rather than the church in terms of the world. In the United States, a good Catholic not only attended the sacraments but engaged socially in a round of activities that immersed them in a parallel society, a social entity that sheltered them from an alien and hostile world. Most Catholics held that social problems could be solved by personal morality, a Christian upbringing, private charity, and close association with the church. It was assumed that religious vocations came from the stable families who externally fit this image of life.

Separation of church and state in this period meant a separation of Christian living and political life. One did not discuss church and politics in polite society, nor in general in religious community. The church and its members shared in public life with others not based on distinctive Catholic tenets of political life but on the basis of commonly shared values and principles which for Catholics were also solidly grounded in faith. The institutional framework for the church's presence in society reflected not only an approach to its mission, but a sense of the church, spirituality, and vision of moral responsibility in the world for its members. People understood their place and their responsibilities in the church. Lay involvement was participation in the apostolate of the hierarchy. Religious life was a hybrid between lay and clergy for those not ordained. The *niche* for religious in practice was linked to their institutional placement and ministry if they were members of active congregations.

Dwight Eisenhower reflected the unifying element of religion and American life in American culture itself. During his presidency, he asserted that the American form of government makes no sense unless it is founded in a deeply held religious faith—whatever it is.[22] *Protestant, Catholic, Jew* by Will Herberg, pointed out how American culture was a melting pot where immigration and American ethnic culture were reflected in its religious movements and institutions.[23] Religious congregations followed these same

---

[22]Paul A. Djupe and Laura R. Olson, *Encyclopedia of American Religion and Politics* (Facts on File Library of American History Series, 2003), 148.
[23]Will Herberg, *Protestant, Catholic, Jew: An Essay in American Religious Sociology* (Garden City, NY: Doubleday, 1955). Yet by 1965, Herberg reflected the

patterns. Over time, each group's internal identity, in many cases, took on a particular flavor from the predominant class or ethnic background of the members who had been recruited through its institutions.[24]

New Catholic Identity and New Understandings of Culture

Vatican II acknowledged that encounter with a culture-free gospel is impossible.[25] Today awareness of a world church brings attention to cultural differences and their impact on the development of faith and its expression. No one who works with teens can ignore that generations have cultures, and these must be understood to communicate. An understanding, however, of changed attitudes toward culture itself is necessary to grasp how these new understandings of culture impact the niche of religious life today.

In the past, cultural theorists imagined a culture, such as church practice, as state, a coherent order in a given culture. Cultures formed a distinctive unit of life and could be identified with a characteristic set of norms, values, beliefs, concepts, dispositions, or preoccupations of a particular people.[26] The elements of a culture were seen as interrelated, providing a form of meaning and order. One could get a "snapshot" of a particular context of living and feel confident in understanding an organization in the wider culture. This was also true of religious congregations. While many congregations founded in the nineteenth century shared a common ethnic background, even commonalities in canon law and ministerial identity—teachers, social workers, or hospital sisters among women; clerical or nonclerical among men—shaped a

---

conservativism of religious culture in America by promoting a gradualist approach to the civil rights movement claiming it was necessary to protect the social cohesion of the country.

[24]Wittberg, *From Piety to Professionalism and Back*, 66.

[25]Gallagher, *Clashing Symbols*, 103.

[26]Judith A. Merkle, *Being Faithful: Christian Commitment in Modern Society* (London: Bloomsbury/T&T Clark, 2010), 84–8.

picture of common life, a niche of religious life, especially before
Vatican II.

Kathryn Tanner in *Theories of Culture: A New Agenda for
Theology* suggests this older cultural theory is no longer adequate
to understand church and culture. Her observations have an impact
on the niche of religious life. In her words:

> It seems less and less plausible to presume that cultures are self-
> contained and clearly bounded units, internally consistent and
> unified wholes of beliefs and values simply transmitted to every
> member of their respective groups as principles of social order.[27]

Instead of a social consensus in which every member of the group
more or less shared, the recognition of pluralism and the cross
pressures of opposite opinions is more realistic. Even if members of
a group declare the same beliefs and values, it is unlikely they will
all mean the same things by them.[28]

Even though every congregation undergoes a certain measure
of consensus building necessary for group identity, the extent of
this consensus is limited. All parties agree on the importance
of the pursuit of a value, even if they do not share a common
understanding of what they mean in all cases. While a congregation,
as the church, needs a coherent system of beliefs and thought which
are foundational for its life to give direction to how a community
adopts, founds, validates, and communicates its Christian life, this
coherence occurs amid many variations.[29]

The coherence is not only in shared beliefs and statements but
in the quality of a congregation's community life. The coherence
is a practical harmony, not just a formal one. Goverance within
a congregation has a unique responsibility in this coherence, but
its responsibility requires all members to discern how to apply the
norms of their shared life in their own contexts.

---

[27]Kathryn Tanner, *Theories of Culture: A New Agenda for Theology* (Minneapolis,
MN: Fortress Press, 1997), 38.
[28]Ibid., 46.
[29]Brian Johnstone, "Moral Methodology," in *The New Dictionary of Catholic Social
Thought*, ed. Judith Dwyer (Collegeville, MN: The Liturgical Press, 2004), 90. For a
congregation, the consensus is often expressed in its constitution.

According to Tanner, norms are cultural forms. Unless human agents struggle over and interpret what the values of their congregations mean in concrete situations, they never become real directives of their shared life. There must be interaction, negotiation, partial steps forward, difference of opinion/fragmentation, and openness to input beyond the boundaries of the congregation for the values of their shared life to impact the real societies in which it is embedded. The "lockstep" image of the shared culture of the pre-Vatican congregation is likely no longer possible, desirable, or effective in the long term; even though its core values remain. This means the culture of religious life is required, in many instances, to interface with secular culture to discern. Instead of having all the answers itself, congregations must ask where love and truth are represented in concrete yet secular form that meet the good of humankind, and then discern how to participate. This is a different cultural model than the model of the mission of the church through the creation of parallel institutions.

The "bundling" of different dimensions of belonging in a more traditional understanding of church culture and that of congregations has been undone. At the same time, there has been an unbundling of another sort. Formerly, the different facets of religious life—liturgy, rites of passage, special devotions, charitable organizations, etc.—were gathered together in the life of a church (locally, within the life of a parish), but this unity too has been "unbundled" and people carry out these activities with different organization and milieu.[30]

These "unbundlings" have been supported in the late twentieth century by the spread of an ethic of authenticity. One version of authenticity promotes a focus on the necessity to "be true to yourself" which is counterposed to engagement in institutions. Keeping one's options open is more culturally appealing then restricting personal choice. Religious life is based on a contrary recognition that self-fulfilment, far from excluding unconditional relationships and moral demands beyond the self, requires these

---

[30]See: *Renewing the Church in a Secular Age: Holistic Dialogue and Kenotic Vision.* Pontificia Universita Gregoriana, Rome, March 4–5, 2015. Proceedings: Council for Research in Values and Philosophy, Co-sponsored by the Pontifical Council for Culture.

in some forms.[31] The "self" meant when we refer to an ethic of authenticity is a "self" formed continuously in interaction with others in the community, not as an island apart from others. These contrasting views of what constitutes human flourishing are aspects of the unbundling of voices which inform the meaning of life in modern society. Individual choice remains an important element in the new niche of religious congregations, as well as communal values contributing to the equilibrium for its stability.

Religious, as all people in the church, no longer share a societal life where all aspects of life reflect the Christian faith. Christians react differently to these changes. Some welcome the freedom and openness and feel free to follow one's spiritual path, as seekers, alongside others who have taken up different positions. Others mourn the passing of an integrated Christian society. The great challenge for the church, as well as religious congregations within it, is to unite believers of both orientations within the church's sacramental union. An insight which flows from these observations is the need for a reappraisal of the meaning of community.

Changed Models of Community

Is community a noun or a verb? If we use the image of a tiger in a cage, is community the cage in which the tiger lives or the energy of the tiger inside the cage? Certainly, the practices of religious congregations before Vatican II emphasized the boundaries of community: who belonged, and who did not; when you could "go out" and when you needed to "be in;" with whom you could associate and with whom you could not. The sociologists of the nineteenth century focused community on geography, common values, ethnic identities, common nationality, and so on. We think of the parishes in the United States of the nineteenth and early twentieth century with neighborhoods with an Italian parish on one corner, German on another, Polish on a third, and Irish on the last. There were Black and white sides of the railroad tracks, marking areas of the city where the other did not travel, and religious orders defined by their

---

[31]Charles Taylor, *The Ethics of Authenticity* (Cambridge, MA: Harvard University Press, 1991).

nationality of origins and divided by race. While these phenomena marked life in America, their dynamics existed across the globe. Today technology forms a type of what people call community. Media, as well as the internet, shift community to both helpful and superficial forms. It can be a link for the good, a support in need, a force of disinformation, and an agent of superficial belonging. The communities of the past or the substitutes of the present are insufficient for the niche of religious life of the future. So where do we turn for models?

The niche of religious life today is challenged by a shift in societal attitudes toward the purpose and place of community in human fulfillment. Modern goals of self-realization imply a purely personal understanding of self-fulfillment, making associations and communities purely instrumental in their significance. Moderns believe our relationships should serve self-fulfillment and in themselves are simply secondary to the self-realization of the partners. A relationship may last over time, perhaps even to death, if it serves its purpose. In this view unconditional ties, meant to last for life, make little sense.[32]

Despite the modern encouragement to "do your own thing" or "find your own fulfilment" people still need intimacy, identity, and support. At times modern society provides for these needs; at others, instead of fostering community it offers some counterfeits, as with lifestyle enclaves.[33] Lifestyle enclaves are not communities. They are groups of people who share similar patterns of consumption, leisure, and interests. In enclaves, people have no common history, memory, or story which gives shape to their lives. Enclaves do not call a group beyond itself. People simply gather around shared preferences, usually leisure and consumption. The morality of the group has no common ideal; it simply reflects the postures of the individuals who form it. The enclave does not have shared practices which cultivate common values to which each member in the group is committed or which mark its goals or purposes. Decisions, if made together, simply conform to whatever is generally practiced in the culture or the convenience of the members. In enclaves there

---

[32]Ibid., 43.
[33]Robert Bellah, *Habits of the Heart: Individualism and Commitment in American Life* (Berkeley, CA: University of California Press, 1985).

are group boundaries, but they are set to keep out others who are not like them. Often, when religious who live in community describe their lives as "living in a hotel," they are describing the drift which has occurred among them to the routines of a lifestyle enclave. Time and again, when people try to establish in a community a "pure relationship" detached from the service of others and attention to the needs of society, they form a type of "enclave" existence.

Community, on the other hand, is a place of manifold engagement. Community is an inclusive whole where people live interdependently with one another, sharing both a private and public life. In community, one generation initiates the next into a way of life. As a center of manifold engagement, community gives each member a significant place in day-to-day participation. Manifold engagement creates important bonds which tie the members together.

Manifold engagement can be contrasted with a lifestyle enclave. Members of a lifestyle enclave are not interdependent, nor do they act together except to ensure the future of their lifestyle together. Their lives are essentially private. Community, on the other hand, is a center of moral formation. Through intact small communities, people learn the staying power and trust to temper themselves, to serve, to sacrifice, to lead, to observe meaningful traditions, to develop character, to practice decision-making, to recover from mistakes, and to forgive. Communities also support people across the life cycle: both taking time with the young and providing care for the elderly. In small communities, people learn how the world works. All these life skills are premised on the fact that some values are worth pursuing and the community stands for their pursuit. Values are not simply significant because they are self-chosen; self-fulfillment is reframed in an understanding of community. Self-realization, in this sense, "depends on the understanding that independent of my will there is something noble, courageous and hence significant in giving shape to my own life."[34] When freedom of choice is linked to a broader horizon of significance, which makes some things worthwhile, others less so, and still others not at all, anterior to choice, the horizon of meaning of community

---

[34]Taylor, *The Ethics of Authenticity*, 39.

emerges. For the niche of religious life this horizon is formed by gospel living as interpreted through one's charism.

Community Today

The niche of religious life today is no longer framed around the community style of the past. Community of the nineteenth century was modern compared to monastic communities. Yet it was still a traditional community. Community solidarity in subsequent times was based on shared ethnicity, territorial identity, and common social class.[35] Theorists of today claim that a shared history, identity, mutuality, plurality, autonomy, participation, and integration mark modern community.[36] These values in a modern community often exist in tension with one another, with each community giving priority to the values which are most suitable to the mission in its context. While we cannot explore all these qualities in detail, an overlook of the emphasis they bring to community today will suggest how they bring new influences to the niche of religious life.

A *shared history* assumes that customs, language, geography, shared events, and crises bond a community more than abstract ideals. A community shares a story through which each member's story is interpreted. Since the moral principles of a community are latent in a community's shared culture, a community's history today must be multicultural, open to movements of people across the globe and its diversity, even if its membership is local. Today religious live in a world church and exist in secular cultures or contexts where Christianity exists alongside other religions or non-belief. This changed niche requires the need to balance openness to secularity with the sharing of faith in community. Members need a place to interpret their experiences, express faith, and their struggle in growth.

---

[35]Larry Rasmussen, *Moral Fragments, Moral Community* (Minneapolis, MN: Fortress Press, 1993), 39.

[36]The following analysis is based on and adapted from the work of Larry Rasmussen, *Moral Fragments, Moral Community*, op. cit. 110 ff., and his use of the work of Philip Selznick, *The Moral Commonwealth, Social Theory and the Promise of Community* (Berkeley, CA: University of California Press, 1992), 183–90, 357–65. This is also developed in more detail in Judith A. Merkle, *From the Heart of the Church: The Catholic Social Tradition* (Collegeville, MN: The Liturgical Press, 2004), 241–65.

Without it, they are forced to remain silent about these essential aspects of their life. Community ceases to be a shared context where they can express and share their relationship with God. As religious are more engaged in the broader society than they were when their mission was expressed primarily through their own institutions, their involvements need to be related to their spiritual journey together.

Shared history alone is not sufficient to bond a community. Aspects of shared history can be pathological. Racism, fundamentalism, and participation in a divided church and nation can taint a religious community with a negative identity. Pope Francis sees the culture of dialogue as an apprenticeship which enables everyone to view others with respect: foreigners, immigrants, and people from different cultures. Dialogue is a form of encounter and an essential element of a healthy community today.[37]

Identity refers to the kind of persons being formed by a community. The formation of identity in a community involves a "we" that does not destroy individuality or foster a group identity which postpones mature adulthood. A community of identity is marked by *responsibility*. Consequences are not lost in scales of action whose range of impact makes no one responsible. Nor does a community drift under the illusion everyone is responsible, and nothing gets done. The call to responsibility of a community fosters in it a sense of *authority*. Authority is not uninhibited power and non-approachable disinterestedness; rather broader responsibility among members focuses the ministry of authority at its appropriate levels and encourages a shared discernment of direction. A practice of obedience, which incorporates a sense of the reciprocity of consciences, qualifies how religious best understand their presence in community. *Subsidiarity* is practiced which directs that nothing is done by a higher authority or larger organization that cannot be done as well as by lower or smaller one.[38] As religious explore the meaning of *synodality*, as a dimension of being church, it will impact the identity of religious community in the future.[39]

---

[37]Pope Francis, *Fratelli Tutti*, chapter six.

[38]Michael E. Allsopp, "Principle of Subsidiarity," in *The New Dictionary of Catholic Social Thought*, ed. Judith A. Dwyer (Collegeville, MN: Liturgical Press, 1994), 927–9.

[39]The "*Sinodo 2021–2023. Per una Chiesa sinidale: comunione, partecipazone, missone*," is the logo of the current synod of the universal church which draws attention to these values affecting the changing niche of religious congregations.

THE NICHE OF RELIGIOUS LIFE

Mutuality is the atmosphere of interdependence and reciprocity in a group. People sense they need one another in some way and gain from cooperating with each other. The reordering of relationships in society involving race, ethnicity, and gender needs a basis in community experience where the skills of such interaction can be learned. The community today which cannot foster this growth will lose its place in a changing world. The feminist community points out that mutuality counters a dominating attitude that others know what is good for women and minorities, without including them in the conversations that define the problems and propose their solutions. Certainly, in the church community today, the role of women is one of the most pressing issues. Mutuality creates a climate of *accountability*. It checks a growing world reality where the weak have no influence on those in charge. It avoids the definition of sex differences to ground differences in power and role, especially in ecclesial decisions. The mutuality between the sexes can be defined so that the biological differences between them overshadow the interpersonal mutuality they should share.[40]

Plurality is the most modern of the characteristics of community. It connotes that people will belong to more than one community at the same time. Modern community is not a totalizing one. Membership in a variety of groups does not threaten a group but enhances it. It extends the community into wider spheres of influence and brings to the community the well-being of family, occupational, environmental, professional, ethnic, and religious groups other than that of its own. While a religious congregation is a primary community, its composition in a new niche has shifted to incorporate various levels of affiliation of others who belong to other primary communities.[41]

Equity is both an ideal and a challenge for a pluralistic community. When there are a plurality of perspectives, lifestyles, and backgrounds, then procedures must be put in place which

---

[40]Christine E. Gudorf, "Mutuality," in *The New Dictionary of Catholic Social Thought*, ed. Judith A. Dwyer (Collegeville, MN: Liturgical Press, 1994), 655. See also: Dawn Nothwehr, *Mutuality: A Formal Norm for Christian Social Ethics* (Eugene, OR: Wipf and Stock, 2005).
[41]See: Judith A. Merkle, *Beyond Our Lights and Shadows: Charism and Institution in the Church* (London: Bloomsbury/T&T Clark, 2016), chapter four, "Primary Charisms: Calling and Postmodern Society-A Church in Transition," 87–113.

respect the level of investment of those of the primary group, yet incorporate fairly and significantly those who participate at other levels. This is especially important as the laity is incorporated into what have been historically "clerical" or "religious" circles. What might have been resolved at the breakfast table in past church or congregational climates must hold to the discipline of clear policies and agreed-upon rules of procedure to be fair. Community, in its new niche, contributes to the changes needed at a societal level as a place to learn how to bridge pluralism to get closer to reality. Advocacy for the inclusion of those generally marginalized from decisions which affect their lives is a ministry goal of many religious congregations.

Autonomy is the ability of a community to develop responsible individuals as it incorporates them into a complex of relationships, which gives them a social self or "we." The challenge of forming a sense of belonging amid diversity of cultures, through internationality of scope or interculturality of membership, is a marker of the new niche of religious congregations.[42] Genuine autonomy is the capacity to foster self-direction that avoids both the illusion of unlimited choices with the group and the brutal crushing effect of the group on the individual. Autonomy in many first-world societies can seem like the only value, "whatever he or she decides." However, it can cloud the reality that other values should also be considered when getting to the heart of what is right or wrong in a decision. The same attitude can be taken over by groups whose sense of independence becomes such a high value that dialogue with others becomes impossible.

In the church, autonomy is nuanced by the principle of *mediation*. Mediation is the belief that created realities mediate the grace of Christ. Autonomy of a religious congregation is not for itself alone, but for the purpose of the wider church. Enough autonomy needs to be respected so that the charism of a group can be expressed, while the very identity of its charism, as a grace for others, calls the group to collaborate in the structures of mediation. Grounding autonomy with the horizon of mediation empowers a group to own

---

[42]Maria Cimperman, RSCJ, Roger P. Schroeder, SVD (eds), *Engaging Our Diversity: Interculturality and Consecrated Life Today* (Maryknoll, NY: Orbis Books, 2020).

its own mediating role in church and society and to contribute its voice.

Sufficiency fosters the autonomy of a community. Sufficiency is the commitment to meet the basic material needs which are appropriate for its operation, and the call to evaluate its own operation in terms of its adequacy to meet the needs it seeks to serve. Life communities have needs which last over the long term and are more serious. Its members rely on them throughout their lifespan. However, material needs are more than money: they involve management structures, personal, and reading the energy of members. Some congregations today are assessing their capacity to offer service in the future and ask if they as a group are sustainable. This calls groups to ask questions which go beyond maintaining the status quo. It may mean entering new structures of organization, merging with other groups, creating new outlets of service, or planning how to hand over their heritage to others. All reflects a continuation of their commitment to be sustainable and to take up their charism in a manner which best serves others.

Communion is the call to integration and is at the heart of the image of the church as *communio*. It is not only our effort to be moral that holds the church together. We can count on the action of the Spirit to take us beyond ourselves when our energies prove to be not enough. Communion balances and mixes the values that norm a religious community in its new niche. No one value alone is a mark of an adequate community, although the values we have discussed are important in identifying the new niche of community today. In cultures across the world, the niche of religious life differs, and the balance of these values will be expressed according to varying contexts. The church as a whole is in a new niche in the world. Each culture will respond to influences of global shifts in its own way.

As we identify some aspects of this new niche of religious congregations we return to a previous question. Has cultural change so impacted religious life that it cannot survive? Has its niche been so disturbed that it "as a species" it will become extinct?[43] Some

---

[43]"There is a good deal of evidence to indicate that unconscious fears of an 'ending to everything' are prevalent among many sectors of the population . . .." Anthony Giddens comments on a more globalized sensation, fueled by fears of nuclear and environmental threats, present in modern society. One wonders if perceptions of the

elements of the new niche of religious life have required it already to restructure its life and mission. However, it is likely the changes ahead will surpass those already attempted. To do this, religious need to identify the deeper resources which stabilize and safeguard the identity of religious life in changing circumstances.

---

future of religious life are touched by these sentiments. See: *Self and Society in the Late Modern Age* (Stanford, CA: Stanford University Press, 1997), 183.

3

Beyond Survival

In nature, life changes and grows beyond death, extinction, and demise. Despite decline, species adapt and develop. A study of ice plants in the deserts of Africa shows how certain species evolve impressive adaptations not only to survive but to prosper in environments with scarce water resources. Water is the medium of life in these environments; nevertheless, the ice plants which were studied have, through a distinctive process of flexing and packing mechanism, called on its own internal hierarchical structures for ongoing life. The plants locked and protected their germination to survive by establishing new patterns from within to absorb water. "Central to their success is a distinctive seed dispersal mechanism in which protective valves open only when sufficiently hydrated with liquid water, thus increasingly the likelihood that seeds will be dispersed under conditions favorable to germination."[1] The adaptive behavior of these ice plants did not require an ideal situation: it emerged in arid and semi-arid environments. It was due to the scarcity of water that specific adaptations surfaced and ensured survival and reproduction. In the end the process generated a new species. By way of analogy, as a thought experiment, is it possible to consider the challenge to religious congregations to adapt to changes in their environment through the lens of this environmental model? Can we identify inner pressures in religious congregations which require an adaptation of their life and sense of mission? Are there elements in the "folded structure" of congregational identities,

---

[1]M. J. Harrington et al., "Origami-like Unfolding of Hydro-actuated Ice Plant Seed Capsules," *Nature Communications* 2, no. 377 (2011), 1–7, at 2.

which provide the stabilization necessary for forward movement and generation of new life in changing circumstances? To gain insight into the adaptations possible for religious congregations today, we will distinguish four elements in religious life which serve both as sources of inner pressure as well as elements of identity in its future. In the following we examine religious life as a bridge between the sacred and the secular, as a religiously focused lifestyle, as a trajectory of becoming holy and finding wholeness, and as a witness to values which matter—the coming of the Kingdom.

A Bridge between the Sacred and the Secular

Along the Atlantic coast of Ireland there are caves/homes which early religious fashioned out of the rock. These believers sought a life apart. They carved stairs in a mountainside which led to elevated dwellings that served as early centers of religious life. These lodgings were created before the great orders came to Ireland in later centuries. While isolated from other settlements, they symbolized a core impulse which undergirds religious life: a desire to form an intentional lifestyle within a wider society, to foster union with God, integrity of life, and service of neighbor. Throughout the centuries, religious have had different postures toward society; they have lived separated from society, within it as reformers and intellectuals, immersed in its social needs, and even fought in the military. Today we question how religious life fits into secular society. While some claim that the Christian or, in our case, religious, do the same things as his or her neighbor but with different motivations, is this solution too simple?[2]

The Christian life, the basis of a religious vocation in the church, is more than living with a different set of motivations. Religious form a type of association within a wider society, yet not a separate society. Most religious engage in altered social relations beyond interactions with the church itself. Religious today have the charge

---

[2]Kathryn Tanner, *Theories of Culture: A New Agenda for Theology* (Minneapolis, MN: Fortress Press, 1997), 122.

to "bring forth charity for the life of the world." Religious influence life both within and outside the church, engage in fields where social decisions are made, and individually and institutionally contribute to helping professions and social services. While the total activity of the life of the church is essential to religious life, their lives engage them both in its ministry and beyond its circles. The idea that religious life attends only to the internal needs of the church is no longer true. Today religious life follows the model of the church itself, as a sacrament of God's presence in the world. While it is difficult to completely distinguish vocations from one another, as whatever one focuses on in one vocation, they also share in some manner with all adult lifestyles in the church. At the same time each vocation in the church possesses dimensions and means which characterize it. In this light, it is possible to highlight how religious life serves as a bridge between the sacred and the secular.

The Sacred and the Secular

The struggle to understand the relationship between the secular and the sacred has gone on for centuries in the church. It is relevant for religious life today, as it serves both as a challenge and as a "folded structure," a stabilizing factor, which is key to its future. St. Augustine, at the time of the Roman Empire, addressed the question of how the sacred and the secular intertwine through his depiction of the two kingdoms. He envisioned the cosmos itself as divided into two realities: the city of God and the city of the earth. The *saeculum* is the realm in which the carriers of the two cities are intertwined.[3] The earthly city has two dimensions and is not limited only to sinful humanity. On the one hand, it is the world, which is profane and rejects God; the realm of the impious and the reprobate. On the other hand, the earthly city is simply the material world; the actual space of life, the empirical city where good and bad mix. The earthly city and its institutions have a moral dimension: they can be better or worse in their service of human life. The care of the *saeculum,* or the realm in which the two cities

---

[3]Robert A. Markus, *Christianity and the Secular* (Notre Dame, IN: University of Notre Dame Press, 2006), 48.

intertwine, has importance for all, believers and nonbelievers alike. It is the real world in which all must live.

Contemporary religious life is one bridge in the church between the sacred and the secular. The involvement of religious congregations in the *saeculum*, the concerns which all share in every context, is the realm where the mystery of God's healing and creating in history is in evidence. It is the focus of the charism of apostolic forms of religious life. Theologian John Haughey remarks that while "charisms are notoriously elusive", we can reflect on some patterns they share with other creativity in history.[4] First, charisms are God's way of building up families, communities, parishes, schools, hospitals, agencies, the church, but also business, neighborhoods, cities, and even international relations. Charisms function where there are human needs. The charisms in the church today, including those of religious congregations, go beyond Paul's mention of them solely in an ecclesial framework (1 Cor. 12:7). Vatican II clarified that charisms are to be expressed in the wider society as well as in the church (AA 3).

Religious life, as one historical legacy of monasticism, belongs to the charismatic structure of the church. Its beginnings in the Christian life gave the church a language to speak of charism not simply as a possession of individuals, a dimension of the church, but as a structure in the church. Early monastic communities were seen as charismatic communitarian expressions within the church and as something new. By the Middle Ages the word charism, translated into Latin in the Vulgate, was often referred to as *gratia* or "grace" or "gift." Theology in the Middle Ages stressed the work of the Holy Spirit to inhabit us, to dwell within, to innovate us, and to make us new. In his study on grace, Thomas Aquinas distinguishes what we know today as charism from other graces or gifts from God mentioned throughout the New Testament. In the *Summa Theologica* he wrote:

According, grace is of two kinds. Firstly, there is the grace by which man himself is united to God and this is called sanctifying

---

[4]John Haughey, "Charisms: An Ecclesiological Exploration," in *Retrieving Charisms for the 21st Century*, ed. Doris Donnelly (Collegeville, MN: The Liturgical Press, 1999), 1–2.

grace (*gratia gratium faciens*). Secondly there is the grace by which one man cooperates with another so that he might be brought back to God. Now this kind of grace is called freely bestowed grace (*gratia gratis data*).[5]

Theologians today are in agreement over the identification of *gratia gratis data* with charism.[6]

The distinction between grace given to sanctify the individual and grace given to foster the common good points to how religious life in the church is both a charismatic structure in the church and a bridge between the sacred and the secular. First, religious provide this bridge through their collaboration in community as both a path to God and service to neighbor. Second their mission is to foster the common good of church, community, and society. Lastly, they serve as a sign or witness to God's creative love in history and society through the Holy Spirit.

The relationship between religious congregations and the *saeculum* is further specified by John Paul II. He identified the bond between church and culture, as marked by transcendence and compenetration.[7] The living out of the charism of a religious congregation is marked by transcendence since it is an unfolding gift from God. Yet its expression in ministry is characterized by compenetration. While essentially religious, it takes on real forms in the everyday life of the church and society. In general, charism functions in the various ministries of the church in its offices, in the services it provides as church to its members and beyond, as well as in the broader mission of the church to the world—thus operating in a totally secular realm. The charism of religious congregations is one expression of the charismatic life of the church, one means by which the church is involved in the daily life of every sociopolitical reality.[8] The identification and fostering of the charisms of religious

---

[5]See: *Summa Theologica*, I, II, 3,4, and II qq. 171–8.

[6]Albert Vanhoye, S.J. "The Biblical Question of 'Charisms' after Vatican II," in *Vatican II: Assessments and Perspectives: Twenty-Five Years After (1962–1987)*, Vol. I, ed. Rene Latourelle (Mahwah, NJ: Paulist Press, 1988), 439–88, at 441.

[7]See: Judith A. Merkle, *From the Heart of the Church: The Catholic Social Tradition* (Collegeville, MN: The Liturgical Press, 2004), 236ff.

[8]Judith A. Merkle, *Beyond Our Lights and Shadows: Charism and Institution in the Church* (London: Bloomsbury/T&T Clark, 2016), 126.

life are important both for members of the church and society, as well as for the mission of the church itself. A religious congregation, though its charism, therefore provides a bridge between the sacred and the secular. This constant in its identity is, to follow our analogy, a "folded structure" of congregational life, as congregations ask themselves how to express their charism in secular culture.

Religiously Focused Lifestyle

Max Weber used the term *virtuosi* to refer to the religious lifestyles of those in most faith traditions, focused on attaining, or helping others to attain, some form of inner spiritual perfection. *Virtuosi,* or a religiously focused lifestyle, serves as the second "folded structure" of congregational identities. It marks the centrality of a religious focus as a characteristic of any formulation of religious life in the future. While *virtuosi* exist in many world religions, its description fits, but is not exhausted by, those who enter religious congregations in Christianity. The reality of the *virtuosi* dimension in religious life is often in evidence in the formation process when people, together with the applicant, ask whether this person has a vocation or a calling to religious life. Understanding the meaning of *virtuosi* today means more than Weber's observations in the nineteenth century, yet his analysis can enrich our grasp of its distinctive nature. The concreteness of a sociological approach helps to bridge the lack of language for religious realities in everyday experience in modern society. This absence creates an ambiguity regarding the religious dimension of life in our social imaginations.

The experience of *virtuosi* today is more pluralistic than in Weber's time. The actual form and content of religious virtuosity manifests itself in widely varied ways across world religions, according to Patricia Wittberg.[9] It can be a temporary lifestyle for every adherent of a tradition or a lifelong commitment for a select minority in another. It can be only for males, or in other religions followed mainly by women. People can be expected to be hermits or wandering pilgrims or live in stable communal settings. They may

---

[9]Patricia Wittberg, *From Piety to Professionalism and Back: Transformations of Organized Religious Virtuosi* (Lanham, MD: Lexington Books, 2006), 4.

be teachers to the spiritually immature or avoid all contact with the outside world. They may be members of the priestly hierarchy or can be excluded because of their *virtuosi* identity. Some religions may include two or more versions of *virtuosi* spirituality, existing sometimes in harmony or in mutual suspicion.

Weber linked virtuosity to the phenomenon of charisma. His use of charisma to identify a societal reality is different from the theological meaning of the term religious would rely on today. For Weber, every society has a center—not defined by geography but by a realm of values and beliefs. Governance protects these symbols and provides meaning for membership—this center can even appear to be sacred. Charisma enters these societal realities in two ways. First, it explains how power can be allotted in society differently from through law and tradition. In the case that charisma legitimates someone's given authority it is because of a certain quality of an individual personality by virtue of which he or she is set apart from the ordinary and treated as if endowed with exceptional powers or qualities. Later this influence seeps into forms of societal life and institutionalized.[10] In the second sense, charisma is less tied to a person and more a force which goes against what is currently the structure. Charisma in this way can be an idea or belief which challenges the status quo. Literally anything perceivable or conceivable by the human mind can become a charismatic object and can, in this sense, change human society.[11] Weber concluded in the nineteenth century that science rather than religion in the modern age legitimates society. Science has a charismatic effect on society through the rationalized processes of thinking it promotes. In contrast, Weber identified religion with magic and thought the rationalization of modern culture was the tool which transcended the backward and magical ways of religion.

Weber's linking of charisma and *virtuosi* stems from his interest in change. In his study of religion, he saw religion as having a transformative effect on society. When it properly functioned, it helped a society adapt to new challenges in its environment. In this sense, religion could be a form of charisma. Weber saw *virtuosi* as

---

[10]Max Weber, *On Charism and Institution Building: Selected Papers*, ed. and intro. S. N. Eisenstadt (Chicago, IL: University of Chicago Press, 1988), xvi–xvii., and 48.
[11]See: Merkle, *Beyond Our Lights and Shadows*, 32–44.

an aspect of this dynamism toward change and adaptation to new circumstances. However, he never identified the source of charismatic power; charisma was a phenomenon with a value-free existence. Charisma for Weber was the superior power some persons have over groups of people. It can apply to good or bad people alike—Hitler or the Pope. While charism holds a central role in Weber's theory of social change, it does not satisfy the theological understanding of charism in religious life. It is only a door to the religious meaning of *virtuosi* within religion and how a religiously-focused life defines religious life.

Weber was an agnostic and not interested in religion itself, rather what makes people act within the changed framework of modern life. He argued that the development of a more rational world, where cause and effect calculation was dominant over big picture world views, led to secularization and disenchantment. In modern times people no longer accepted worldviews explained by ideas beyond a means and end calculation, or efficiency—they were no longer "fooled." Religion, in his mind, belonged to this broader meaning system and was simply magic: what he called enchantment. The possibility of symbolic action between God and humans was ruled out; human action could only be secular. For instance, Catholic sacramental practice was seen as an enchanted form of action.[12] The secularization of human action separated the sacred realm of the grace of salvation from the profane realm of human action.[13] Eventually grace itself was eclipsed in his view of modern life.

The Catholic tradition of grace depicts the God–human relationship differently. Grace forms the basis of religious life as *virtuosi*, a religiously focused lifestyle. The root idea of *charis* or charism means God's action in humanity leading us to union with God, not just for *virtuosi* but for everyone. Human action and divine action are not contradictory but ordered to cooperate together in living a virtuous life. Nature is "all that which is not God" yet human nature remains radically open to God.[14] German

---

[12]Max Weber, "The Different Roads to Salvation," in *On Charisma and Institutional Building*, 268–78.
[13]Anthony J. Carroll, S.J., *Weber, Secularization and Protestantism* (Scranton and London: The University of Scranton Press, 2007), 87. For disenchantment, see 87–94.
[14]For a fuller description of the "world" in its role in the Christian life see: Judith A. Merkle, *Being Faithful: Christian Commitment in Modern Society* (London: T&T Clark, 2010), 22–36.

sociologist Hans Joas remarks that Weber's incorporation of charisma into his interpretation of society is helpful only to a point. It is not supported by a theory of action which accounts for it.[15] For Joas, creativity in society is a marker of charisma or charismatic action: a type of action that goes beyond the two main reasons people act. One is rational action, which has a purpose, and the other is normative action, as a response to a sense of right and wrong. Creative action incorporates the two yet goes beyond them and has its own spark of newness. The transformative effect of Francis of Assisi on the church, or the impact of Therese of Lisieux on spirituality; the martyrdom of Romero, or the witness of the Nagasaki martyrs; the impact of the teaching and nursing congregations on post-Industrial Revolution generations, cannot be explained through rational or normative action alone. Charles Taylor comments that the common perception which identifies religion with enchantment also transformed the general practices of religion itself. We have moved from an era in which religion was more "embodied," where the presence of the sacred could be enacted in ritual, seen, felt, touched, and walked toward (in pilgrimage), into one which is more "in the mind." In his words, ". . . our link with God passes more through our endorsment of contested interpretation—for instance, of our political identity as religiously defined, or of God as the authority and moral source underpinning our ethical life."[16] Response to the grace which defines the God-human encounter lies at the heart of the religiously focused lifestyle of religious life.

The meaning of how religious life is an expression of *virtuosi* behavior not only must go beyond Weber but to a deeper look at the nature of religion itself. If religion is not just an escape into a magical or infantile existence, then what motivates a human choice moved by a religious desire? It is important to examine this experience to better understand how religious life is, and needs to remain, a religiously focused lifestyle in secular times.

---

[15]Hans Joas, *The Creativity of Action*, trans. Jeremy Gaines and Paul Keast (Chicago, IL: University of Chicago Press, 1996).
[16]Charles Taylor, *A Secular Age* (Cambridge, MA: The Belknap Press of Harvard University Press, 2007), 554.

Religious Desire

Religion can appear to be one choice among others. The age-old charge that religion "creates" pride through an assumption of moral superiority to others is fueled by the notion that religion is a choice, like any other choice. In the context of a consumer society, religious identity can seem like one choice among others—a preference for a style of faith, or a selection among options.[17] On the contrary, Hans Joas argues that the will which responds to religion is distinguishable conceptually from a rational choice between preferences. Faith is itself a state of grace: humans can aspire to it, but cannot coerce it.

Religious faith is based either on traditions internalized in the process of self-formation or on experiences of self-transcendence.[18] An experience of self-transcendence is the experience of being moved beyond the self by another, a situation, or a personal recognition of something of which one was previously unaware. The will expressed in this situation is one of surrender. One is now in a new place, experienced as a better self, a truer self, or a hidden self that is not as positive as once thought but is integrated into a fuller sense of self—as one measures by a different standard. There is an element of passivity in this experience as well as affirmation. One is moved or seized by something; one experiences a self-surrender to "more."

While people know they have experienced something religiously, they often do not know what it means. Religious experience is not something which flows from previous cultural or religious interpretive patterns. Rather it demands continued interpretations to be meaningful to people of the times. We see in the history of religious communities that generations interpret traditions, establish new connections, and devise new, creative articulations or religious innovations. A community over time develops a framework of interpretation of religious experience as they live their vocation in changing circumstances.

William James describes the faith of a religious person not as holding something to be true in the cognitive sense, a belief that

---

[17]See: Vincent Miller, *Consuming Religion: Christian Faith and Practice in a Consumer Society* (New York: Continuum, 2004).

[18]Hans Joas, *Do We Need Religion?* trans. Alex Skinner (London: Paradigm, 2008), 29.

might be shaken by discursive argument, but rather as an attitude toward reality underpinned by the sure sense that a greater power is present. Like someone who falls in love, the beloved affects one's life, even when not physically present.[19] The same is true of conversion and prayer. Both are marked by a non-volitional character since it is a communication with the power from which the individual's life force flows. One does not create this power, rather one touches into it and is moved by it. Prayer in this sense is a witness that something real is there.[20] It is a power which cannot be forced but must be allowed to graciously reveal itself.

Values

Values, on the other hand, and religious values specifically, are not long-term preferences or preferences of a higher order but reflexive standards by which we evaluate our preferences. They are like the "transcendent data" we use to weigh our preferences.[21] These emotionally-laden ideas of what is desirable come from our important relationships in life. Value commitments do not arise from rational arguments about what is better or best, but from experiences of self-formation and self-transcendence. These are the experiences that push people beyond the self and contribute to their sense of what is "good." Over the course of our lives, we must put faith in people to learn from them. We observe how their values have brought them satisfaction in life. We take on the practices which form those values in our own lives. We internalize what we have learned and try out what we have observed. Our sense then of what is "good" is based on self-evidence and affective intensity.[22]

The *virtuosi* experience of a religious vocation is centered in the example of living the gospel by the Christian community, ritualized

---

[19]William James, *The Varieties of Religious Experience* (Cambridge, MA: Harvard University Press, 1985), 66.

[20]Ann and Barry Ulanov, *Primary Speech: A Psychology of Prayer* (Louisville, KY: Westminster John Knox Press, 1982), 126.

[21]Juan Luis Segundo, *Faith and Ideologies*, trans. John Drury (New York: Orbis, 1984), 73.

[22]Hans Joas, *The Genesis of Values*, trans. Gregory Moore (Chicago, IL: University of Chicago Press, 2000), 85.

in the liturgy, celebrated in the sacraments, mediated through the church, and anchored in a tradition of witnesses, saints, martyrs, prophets, teachers, theologians, leaders, and advocates for justice. It is more than a moral choice: it is an expansion of horizons as to what human life is for, if God is in it. For the individual religious it is an encounter with their life purpose. As we will see later in our discussion of the vows, for one with a religious vocation, the centrality of one's relationship with God is primary in the interpretation of its meaning. The perception of a call is an experience of being moved by the Real beyond oneself. Acknowledgment of it is an entry into a journey—one's own transformation to fulfillment. It is a choice to follow one's spiritual path in the shaping of one's own autobiography in community with others. The wholeness to which God calls and restores in the individual is also a renewed oneness with all humankind. Julian of Norwich alludes to this in her writing: "The love of God creates in us such a unity that, when it is truly seen, no man can separate himself from another."[23] This *virtuosi* experience, recognition of a calling from God, interpreted through the community of the church remains a "folded structure" of congregational identities, essential for its further growth and development. At its core, it defines religious life as a religiously focused lifestyle, yet one intrinsically united with love of neighbor.

Trajectory of Becoming Holy—Finding Fullness

A trajectory is a path forward. In our case it is a path to find God, the third "folded structure" of congregational identities. The concept of a path forward, which can be travelled by many, beyond the creation of an individual, meets special problems in the modern era. Theologian James Fowler describes the path to adulthood imagined in former times as "building a tent." The transition to adult living involved creating a "tent" for life, with pegs comprising

---

[23]Julian of Norwich, *Showings*, ed. Edmund College and James Walsh, The Classics of Western Spirituality (New York: Paulist Press, 1978), 309; as quoted in Mary Frohlich, *Breathed into Wholeness: Catholicity and Life in the Spirit* (New York: Orbis Books, 2019), 190.

a place to live, a profession or career, and a life partner. In modern society life is visualized differently. Each life is so individualized and unique that choices are made apart from paths others have taken, and independent from the institutions which have directed and shaped life in other periods. Former paths may be viewed even as an obstacle to true flourishing.[24]

In contrast, modern society offers many lifestyles to choose from. The "nova effect" of modern life is the explosion of ethical, religious, and atheistic options which surround us as possibilities for a meaningful life. Common to the secular vision is an eclipse of all goals beyond human flourishing, as all that is worth one's effort rests on the "natural scope" of life—the passage of birth to death.[25] A life without God in the picture is conceivable for masses of people. The challenge of life when understood only in an immanent frame is coupled often with disbelief in the people and institutions which offered a life map in the past centuries. The fact the church today struggles with its own loss of authority through the sexual abuse crisis contributes to the disconnection people have with it as a guide for life. This situation adds to the confusion as to how religious life offers an adult path of becoming to people today.

Charles Taylor sees there are reoccurring challenges believers face in finding a trajectory of holiness throughout history. Every age seeks how to restore a previously established, then grievously challenged, church order in new circumstances. No generation grasps the whole picture of a totally right understanding of Catholic Christianity. While people either espouse a progressive or traditional view, none can grasp alone everything that participates in human alienation from God.[26] The tendency of every generation is to assume there is only one single paradigm of church order, whether it is found in some past era (traditionalists) or in the present age (progressives). Taylor argues that both approaches hide the rich variety of paths to God which exist simultaneously in every age. We observe that people today often "lean toward" one of these paradigms. Yet religious congregations are challenged to be vital by

---

[24]James Fowler, *Becoming Adult, Becoming Christian: Adult Development and Christian Faith* (San Francisco, CA: Jossey-Bass, 2000), 1–13.
[25]Taylor, *A Secular Age*, 20.
[26]Ibid., 765–6.

keeping before the church community "paradigm itineraries" which cannot be identified with those of any one age. I remember having a conversation with a colleague in a male religious order. He said as he aged how grateful he was to have joined his community. It was big enough and broad-minded enough to integrate even a character like himself! The communion of saints, each life offering a trajectory of holiness, contains different postures, personalities, professions, and practices as "paths to God." The conversion process offered by any itinerary of the Christian life involves the discovery of new ways to move beyond the present orders to God offered by both the "left" and the "right" in the culture wars of the church. It is only then one can seek the real goal, union with God, in Godself.

Taylor offers an example of how a new trajectory shows itself in the modern era. Therese of Lisieux is an exemplar of the secular age as her path to God transverses the modern condition. In an earlier age, people were considered "sinners" who lived with only a faint sense of God and Christ, without really relating to Him. Everyone, the whole society, was both sinner and engaged in the act of believing. Life depended on God. Today we live in a world in which the negation of God is a real option, adopted by millions. Therese experienced this lack of faith. In her spiritual life, she shared with Christ this sense of how goodness, especially in Christ's person, is rejected and ignored. But it did not lead her to close herself off from this pain of realization or disconnect with others who did not share her faith. Her aim was to live in it, wanting to believe in its midst, and to be with God. This was her "little way."[27] Given the complexities of the spiritual journey today, we can ask what constants in religious life make it a trajectory of holiness, a constant, as a "folding structure" of congregational life?

A Community of Interpretation

Karl Rahner claims that when people are moved by the Real beyond themselves in faith, the experience needs to be interpreted. Belief in God needs to be named and given a framework. Faith in God, as personal and mysterious as it is, is always entered into

---

[27]Ibid., 850, note 64.

historically, in a time and a place, and in a community which can help us find its meaning in our lives. A consequence of being human is that we seek God and pursue mystery through rituals, rites, dogmas, and prayers.[28] We do not do so just in our minds, or move forward aimlessly through vague urgings. The only way to enter one's own transformation is to take a path, a trajectory, in time, which brings the whole of ourselves into this process. If God shares God's Self through revelation and scripture then one must ask, where is the group in time that lives by this reality?[29]

Life in the church is inseparable from religious life. Even though current problems in the church make this posture conflictual for some, Taylor reminds us that standing in the church has been a continual challenge throughout history. As human beings, no one of us can find our way to God alone, yet we try. From time to time, people stand out because they have grasped some powerful key to this journey in their time. Religious identify the founders or foundresses of their congregations, as well as individuals in their congregational history, as among these witnesses. With these signature individuals, and the communion of saints, people are introduced to a life in God lived more fully than individuals could live alone. Straining to understand these voices, deeper than the current polemic, religious live their congregational charism and find focus in it. Through this grounding they can be open to receive contemporaries who too might walk to a "different drum." Religious can allow intercultural experience to stretch their understanding of life and develop their capacity to meet diversity and its goodness in new ways. The faith of any generation is not the acme of Christianity, nor is it a degenerate version. A religious community witnesses a process of conversation in understanding the meaning of the Christian life which extends over centuries. The fragmentary experience of any congregation is not seamless. We can learn from those in the past and present since they are not perfect people. But they are those who, like us, could not leave their imperfections behind them, who rather took them along in living a whole life—offering to those who follow

---

[28]Declan Marmion, *A Spirituality of Everyday Faith: A Theological Investigation of the Notion of Spirituality in Karl Rahner* (Louvain: Peeters Press, 1998), 57.
[29]Juan Alfaro, "Faith," in *Sacramentum Mundi*, ed. Karl Rahner, Vol. 2 (London: Burns and Oates, 1968), 313.

itineraries to God. In the whole journey of the communion of saints rests the accomplishments, the betrayals, the mistakes, the outreach, the excesses, and the rejections inherent to the human condition. We learn how God makes all these human passages stepping stones to Godself, and the meaning which emerges through them. This realism helps us interpret our own journey personally and as a congregation.

While membership in the church is a primary "hermeneutic of interpretation" of the life of a religious, the charism of the congregation and its witness throughout history is another. Religious life witnesses a particular feature of the development of charism, not attested to in the New Testament. It reflects how charism can affect numerous people over extended periods of time. Instead of charism seen only as a gift given to an individual for the good of the church, charism is also a tradition which impacts people, over generations. The development of institutes of consecrated life fashioned in the church's new patterns whereby the spiritual and apostolic orientations received from the founder or foundress of a congregation were passed on to members of the institute. This not only impacted the church at large but could be interpreted for and by those who lived in different states of life. The example of the "little way" of St. Therese of Lisieux, the creation of St. Vincent de Paul societies, or Third Order movements of the Franciscans and other congregations are expressions of this shared life. Today this extension of itineraries to the broader church lived in other Christian lifestyles continues to develop the charismatic life in the church.[30] Congregations today are experimenting with various associations with the laity in animating the renewal of the church, mutually supporting, and being enriched by lay charisms in various professions, lifestyles, and adult commitments.

A Framework for Becoming in Secular Society

A religious vocation involves engagement with mystery and the transcendent: two dimensions of life which secular society overlooks. The public dimension of religious life witnesses a quality

---

[30]Merkle, *Beyond Our Lights and Shadows*, 1–27 at 24.

of life which is not simply a religious legitimation of the values of the society in which it lives.[31] In this sense, a religious community is a moral community. The term moral suggests a posture toward what it means to be human and to act on that knowledge, and what is necessary for human community to flourish. In the past, moral issues were seen as having to do mainly with personal conduct within stable orders of value.[32] Today a moral community must include a new sense of responsibility, a posture toward the issues which have to do with the life or death of humanity as such, and the fate of the created order in which we live.[33] A religious congregation attests to a framework for becoming, both the individual and the society in which it exists. This capacity to witness a scaffolding of personal and social development, as a life group, is an aspect of the third "folded structure" of congregational identities. This stable element of congregational life offers both an avenue for congregational renewal and signifies a key element in adaptation as a life structure in changing circumstances.

Bernard Lonergan explains why a framework of life is necessary for personal development. In first-world culture, we tend to see human development as personal effort alone, simply a matter of taking responsibility to use our talents and shape our choices. However, Lonergan in his article "Healing and Creating in History," sees a life framework as having two fundamental and complementary directions.[34] One way is the way of achievement. The other is more receptive, the way of heritage and consciousness of the goodness which comes into one's life. The first way, based on Lonergan's theory of knowing, begins with an attentive experience of information. It moves to a critical reflection on one's understanding, and from this critical reflection to responsible decisions. This path of personal development occurs not only in the life of the individual religious but also in congregations. Religious congregations, as a

---

[31]James Cone, *Speaking the Truth: Ecumenism, Liberation and Black Theology* (Grand Rapids, MI: Eerdmans, 1986), 118.

[32]See: Merkle, *Being Faithful*, chapter one, "Living into a New Paradigm," 3–21.

[33]Lewis S. Mudge, *The Church as Moral Community: Ecclesiology and Ethics in the Ecumenical Debate* (New York: Continuum, 1998).

[34]Bernard Lonergan, "Healing and Creating in History," in *The Lonergan Reader*, ed. Mark D. Morelli and Elizabeth A. Morelli (Murray) (Toronto: University of Toronto Press, 1997), 106.

life group, heal and create in history by interpreting the signs of the times and responding through responsible decision-making.

The second way of development is of heritage; one's education, family, security of nation, and so on. From these experiences of upbringing and socialization we form a mindset, a worldview, or horizon as to what life is about. In his words, "There is the transformation of falling in love: the domestic love of the family, the human love of one's tribe, one's country, mankind; the divine love that orientates man in his cosmos and expresses itself in worship."[35] Through the integration of the two sources of development on a personal level, with their gifts and limitations, we slowly become our own masters, think for ourselves, make our own decisions, and exercise our own freedom and responsibility.[36] A religious congregation enters into this same process, through remembrance of its own history and interpretation of charism, fosters this integration in its members, and becomes a context for this process to occur over a lifetime.

A religious congregation is a framework for becoming where this integration takes place. As a life group, it contains patterns of cooperation, commonly understood ways of proceeding, ways of arriving at common consent, and supporting a common life. Each generation in a congregation reframes what it has received either positively or negatively. Positive development cannot be accomplished by group membership alone. It requires the desire to be authentic on the part of members and the group. For Lonergan authenticity is the consistent struggle to be attentive, intelligent, reasonable, and responsible. It requires the ability to prioritize, as individuals and as groups. In the crossroads of choice, it calls for decision and action. Is this worth my effort, our effort, how do I or we begin?

A final piece in this sketch of Lonergan's approach to development is how individuals and groups can cripple their capacity to grow. Bias is a major block to the flourishing of an individual or group. Lonergan does not see bias as the only force which limits growth,

---

[35]Ibid.
[36]Bernard Lonergan, "The Ongoing Genesis of Methods," in *A Third Collections: Papers by Bernard J. F. Lonergan, S.J.*, ed. Frederick E. Crowe (New York: Paulist Press, 1985), 156.

but he does carefully delineate its dynamisms—which are easily recognized in communal life. There is the bias of individual egoism which limits an individual's questioning to only those things which contribute to his or her, or a group's own point of view. Group egoism is corporate blindness used by a group to ignore a situation, fail to deal with the problem, or dismiss a remedy simply because it could limit its power. Finally, there is general bias or the insistence on immediate results, which steers an individual or a group to forsake working toward values and goals which are long in coming.

The charism of a religious congregation is a factor in the process of individual and group becoming. An individual "becomes" through a growth in personal interiority and consciousness of and response to the world and its needs. A deepening and recognition of the community as a chosen framework of becoming, and as a personal context for life and mission in church and society also develops. Attention to charism can foster in a group an outward outlook and animate desire to read the signs of the times. It can summon the group to effectively communicate a sense of transcendence within a secular society, and to shape the institutions in which they are involved in a manner which is conducive to human becoming. In this sense, religious congregations are not only frameworks for becoming holy and finding fullness themselves but foster this development in the service they offer to others. This aspect of religious life forms a "folded structure" of congregational identities and is essential for its further renewal. At its core, it defines religious life as offering a trajectory of becoming holy and finding fullness.

Witness to What Matters—the Kingdom

A secular society offers many reasons to act. Beyond the different reasons people call upon to do their daily tasks, they also have different interpretations as to why they search for the "more" of life. Taylor calls this deeper purpose the drive toward fullness. We see our lives, and their course over time, as having a certain moral/spiritual shape. We imagine the direction of our lives as a move forward. "Somewhere, in some activity, or condition, lies a fullness, a richness, that is, in that place (activity or condition), life is fuller richer, deeper, more worthwhile, more admirable, more what it should be."[37] Usually, life goals of fullness are seen as health, wealth, family, education, career, and the like. Religious share these goals, but also have other values which shape their priorities. Desire for union with God, attention to mission, and the promotion of the good of the community and society impact the meaning they give to fullness and their priorities. Over time, many of our aspirations are challenged by experiences which do not match expectations. Life throws us a curve, and what results is an experience of exile. Whatever interpretation placed on life, ideas of fullness, or the means to reach it, is contradicted often by a contrary experience. These contradictions create a situation of tension in every life. Inevitably, we meet those whose lives exhibit fullness on another basis or we encounter an alternative model of fullness which distracts us. Constant exposure to the range of options to fullness, and multiple paths to find it, plunge moderns into what Charles Taylor calls the "cross pressures of transcendence and immanence:" a condition of doubt and uncertainty between the search for "more" and living in the here-and-now.

Religious and their congregations face this same challenge. Amid the explosion of options and explanations of a meaningful life they seek a framework of living that combines the daily and the eternal. They seek to respond to the coming of the Kingdom of God in the real world. They live in the tension of the "already" and the "not yet" of the Kingdom. Confronting the gap between what is and what ought to be challenges them to make decisions. Religious cannot retreat into a life of personal perfection set apart from the concerns of humanity. Even though they live side-by-side with those who might see all goals beyond human flourishing as meaningless, they beg to differ. Their lives rest on the belief that the Kingdom does come in their midst. Religious share deeply the affirmation of Karl Rahner that the capacity to find God in one's life, everyday mysticism, is key to the future of the church for all Christians and for their congregations.[38] They struggle, in their own lifestyles and congregational lives, to promote and grow in this contemplative

---

[37]Taylor, *A Secular Age*, 5–20 at 5.
[38]Karl Rahner, "The Spirituality of the Church of the Future," in *Theological Investigations*, Vol. 20 (London: Darton, Longman and Todd, 1981), 148.

awareness. They seek to witness to a life based on awareness of God as its center, avoiding both retreat into a false withdrawal or a surrender to total assimilation into the secular landscape. This fourth constant in religious life, being a witness to what matters— the values and the coming of the Kingdom—stands within the context of secular life. It is essential both to the ongoing renewal and the future of religious life.

Values Worth the Effort

If we look at the history of religious life, we find vibrant contributions to the best of what society offered during a historical period, as well as a critique of cultural norms not in keeping with the gospel. Despite failures in religious life and its need for reform, it has borne witness to gospel values throughout history. The early hermits fled the decadence of the Roman Empire; the Franciscans challenged the drive for power and riches within the church and medieval society. The Beguines of the Middle Ages offered service to and life among the poor and those who needed them, rather than the security of life apart. Communities during and after the Reformation met the needs of new populations for education, health care, and social services. All were witnesses to constitutive values, as values worth the effort, in every period.

As religious today meet this task in secular society they face new challenges. The secular situation does not necessarily give rise to an absence of ethics, rather to a new ethic without religious grounding. Moderns believe in human dignity and universal benevolence but generally hold that neither goal needs aid from a transcendent source.[39] Men and women today often are not in touch with the moral sources which originally underpin these standards. The original Christian source is *agape*, the love God has for humans, which relates to their goodness as creatures.[40]

Secular society offers a new moral order which is independent of any claims about God. The modern moral order is one of

---

[39]Charles E. Curran, *The Social Mission of the U.S. Catholic Church: A Theological Perspective* (Washington, DC: Georgetown University Press, 2011).
[40]Judith A. Merkle, *Discipleship, Secularity and the Modern Self: Dancing to Silent Music* (London: Bloomsbury/T&T Clark, 2020), 56, 86.

working in society for mutual benefit. While not a total break from religion, behind these values is a vague notion of a providential God, detached from any tradition. This deity keeps a distance from human life and has little impact on concrete affairs. The delinking of providence from any spiritual tradition or interpretative framework gives a nod to what is ultimate and transcendent but renders it both irrelevant and "authoritative" at the same time. What emerges is an ethic which affirms a mode of self-sufficient social living, which is an end in itself. The norm of "mutual benefit" often gets reduced to a practice of the status quo.[41] The divine, in this system, can no longer challenge. A task facing religious in secular society is to counter the delinking of God, ultimate purpose, and societal norms in secular life.

Not all links between Christianity and political and social life, however, are constructive. There are many forms of false versions of Christianity in global societies with political overtones which are oppressive. One interpretation translates Christianity into a form of white Christian nationalism which threatens democracy, excludes minorities, and sanctions violence, all in the name of liberty, property, and rights.[42] Here the language of Christianity is used, while its essence and normative challenge is manipulated. Secularity can set the stage for this to occur. When humans alone make this world meaningful, humans can shrink the goal and shift the source of moral/spiritual resources to the here-and-now alone. When this world is all there is, moral fullness and our highest moral capacity and inspiration is focused solely on our intra-human powers.[43] Without awareness of the significance of the transcendent, the Word of scripture, the tradition of faith, and the community of conscience, religion can morph into a tool of oppression rather than a source of healing—a designer project without a soul. Religious are called to witness the values of the Kingdom in the face of this climate. Religious do witness climates of lawlessness, persecution, and unthinkable oppression across the world: they accompany migrants, receive orphans, bring health care to the marginated, teach the ignorant and

---

[41]Taylor, *A Secular Age*, 237–9.
[42]Philip S. Gorski and Samuel L. Perry, *The Flag and the Cross* (Oxford: Oxford University Press, 2022).
[43]Taylor, *A Secular Age*, 244–5.

face expulsion or imprisonment, and torture themselves on account of their advocacy of others. Religious congregations, however, can also mirror the racism and tribalism that plague societies. Witness to the Kingdom involves a desire to do what is necessary to both affirm and critique social forms according to how they promote the human and the values of the gospel. Religious do work side-by-side in society with those who uphold this normative outlook, even without explicit religious identity. The fact that explicit religious identity is not part of the life journey of some does not detract from the importance of the contribution of religious and their discernment of what matters in the complexity of these times.

Maximal Demand and the Human Trap of Self-Sufficiency

At first glance, the societal standards which encourage moderns to be concerned for the life and well-being of all human beings globally seem positive. Christians concur people are to further social justice and subscribe to universal standards of human rights. They are to care for the earth. The compatibility between these standards, and those of believers, prompts people to wonder: if there are good people everywhere, does being religious have any purpose?

However, people question whether a self-sufficient morality exacts a high price from humans in terms of wholeness. Are these moral standards alone compatible with the human fulfillment they promise? What happens when high ideals stand in conflict with other life goals? Recognition that "all is not well with the world" spurs efforts among good people to change it. Yet, Taylor asks, without a power greater than ourselves, can our highest spiritual or moral aspirations crush or mutilate what is essential to our humanity?[44]

Today the moral obligations which people face are beyond those held in previous generations. When human efforts fail, or their success uncovers a further challenge which seems insurmountable, how do people go on? There are incidences of suffering in the world which appear to have no redeeming value. Where do we go with the

---

[44]Ibid., 639–40.

dead ends that war, famine, epidemics, and hunger leave us if we admit their existence and impact on our world?[45]

The core question at the heart of an ethic framed only in the immanent frame is whether anything more than a "well lived" life is needed for happiness. Are all solutions within the reach of the human community? Religious are called to live a life which recognizes both the contingency of human existence: we need God, as well as the capacity of modern life to create solutions to meet the challenges of our times. They are asked to attest that human initiative and creativity are not an affront to God and that, at the same time, cooperation with God does not diminish one's humanity.

The central value in a secular cultural framework is choice as a supreme value—irrespective of what it is a choice between or in what domain. The notion of choice, singled out from other values, does not address the sacrificial alternatives in a dilemma or the moral weight of any situation. Am I required to sacrifice for another? Is their need more important than mine? These questions are not solutions to problems; they are the value issues which undergird the possibility a problem will even be addressed. When religious are called to witness to the values of the Kingdom, they are summoned to stand for the truths of human life which often determine whether there is the political will to address the problem at all. They witness to our need for God, our reliance on one another, and our connection to the earth. These values impact the realm of possibility that a moral solution can be found. The counterpart of a world of choice is tolerance—each one does their own thing and is respectful of the values of each person.[46] But where does this ethic lead? Concerns around the privacy of the individual can erode even legal traditions. When the supremacy of choice is the sole determiner of right and wrong, the problem is not with the solution, the problem is with the vision of living which undergirds it. Even citizens forget that, in the democratic ideal, the pursuit of life, liberty, and happiness is always considered within a framework of character and values which are assumed in citizenship.[47] Religious life is one way the Christian life

---

[45]Merkle, *Discipleship, Secularity and the Modern Self*, 186–8.
[46]Taylor, *A Secular Age*, 478.
[47]See: David Hollenbach, *Humanity in Crisis: Ethical and Religious Responses to Refugees* (Washington, DC: Georgetown University Press, 2019).

is made explicit in its testimony to what is human, in contrast to a secular framework of life's meaning.

Without a holistic vision of human life, another societal danger arises: a type of moralism. Moralism is a legalism which overemphasizes the moral code in the Christian life; fidelity is measured solely by external practices in the personal realm. In the public realm, predetermined public conformity to the letter of the law replaces an informed conscience which addresses the mixed goods in societal life. Moralism avoids the question of the meaning of human life and the behavior which flows from it. Christian ethics is more than quandary ethics, offering only "answers" to current moral dilemmas. Rather it attends to the controlling narrative within which one learns to identify a moral question or topic at all and search for its solution.[48] The drift toward legalism is not a move toward the values of the coming of the Kingdom of God. It replaces a mature development of conscience and an openness to the process of real conversion. Today the "light" such moralism provides is often measured by political correctness, party conformity, or shallow thinking. The question of what is rewarded or challenged is resolved more by who is doing it, not the content or value of what they are doing. Tolerance can be reduced to inaction and an erosion of mutual respect, which leaves real needs unaddressed. The result is an impasse between groups who simply seek to tolerate one another without generating positive action to address the institutional roots of problems which plague society, the global community, and, in some cases, congregations. All forms of moralism lead more to concern about "being right" than "doing right." Citizens can leave immigrants and aliens without recourse and, at the same time, feel justified in a procedural correctness which is institutional abandonment in practice.

Religious after Vatican II often have been called to be prophetic. It is unlikely that every religious is prophetic. However, their congregations should be. Their witness to the Kingdom can neither be an acquiescence to the illusions and anxiety of maximal demand, nor a watering down the meaning and challenge of the gospel to make it more palatable to modern sensibilities. This "cheap grace,"

---

[48]Dallas Gingles, "Narrative," in *T&T Clark Handbook of Christian Ethics,* ed. Tobias Winright (London: Bloomsbury/T&T Clark, 2021), 103–10.

as Dietrich Bonhoeffer would state it, is not their witness for the life
of the world. Nor does it go deep enough to attract others to give
their lives to a religious calling. There is a wholeness of religious
life which in its own way attests to values which really matter. To
meet the moral questions which arise in so many different contexts
across the world, religious need to recognize that the values of
their own lifestyle are important to witness to what matters—the
Kingdom—in face of these challenges.

Religion Which Makes a Difference

Religion and religious life threaten the order of mutual benefit
through the promotion of self-restraint. Religion holds that material
desires can be satiated. In contrast, modern society assumes a
"theory of progress:" the claim that the modern economy, propelled
by human greed, holds the secret of progress; the desires of one
generation become the necessities of the next. Religion, on the
other hand, holds that material desires are not limitless. Religion
calls for the possibility of directing sensual pleasure and the erotic
impulse to other human goals of relationship and family. Religious
witness that a celibate sexual lifestyle leads neither to frustration
nor isolation and challenges an unqualified trust in natural
instinct. This does not call everyone to celibacy, but it does affirm
the possibility of meaningful sexual expression in every lifestyle.
Religion holds to an idea of prosperity which involves a broader
sense of relationships than economic ones alone; it fosters solidarity
and care for the earth.

Witness to the values of the Kingdom involves constitutive
goods. Constitutive goods are not the same as life goods. In the
mix of personal goals, desires, and hopes for our life course,
there are "strong evaluations": the recognition that certain goals
or ends make a claim on us and are incommensurable with our
other desires and purposes.[49] The life and works of a religious
congregation are based not only on the consequences of its action
in its good works but also on the source in their life stance. The

---

[49]This application of Taylor is explained in Merkle, *Discipleship, Secularity and the
Modern Self*, 147–9.

works of a congregation are socially useful and therefore serve the common good; they can be done excellently and thus have status in educational or healthcare professions; they are economically productive and support members and good works. Yet, all do not override the foundational reasons they exist and why they stand by certain values and actions. "The love of Christ compels us" (2 Cor. 5:14). The turn to this higher norm in light of their charism is a compass for the congregation. It can check the moral being reduced to the economic. It can support members to pull back the notion of mutual benefit from serving a privileged few. It can move people to transcend existing solidarities of race, class, gender, and nationality to welcome their neighbor in need. It can call to action a society which protests a high degree of philanthropic action yet is crippled by a minimum hope in humankind itself and fears humans may destroy the earth on which we rely. Religious congregations, by bearing witness to the narrative upon which their lives are based, can contribute to these important values that animate secular society. They can do so even in face of dissenting voices who assert these goals can be reached through human initiative alone. This witness to "values worth the effort," or constitutive goods, the values of the gospel and the Kingdom, is central to religious life and serves as a folded structure in its framework of becoming. It expresses how religious congregations share in the mission of the church as a sacrament of God's love for the world. It is their witness to what matters, values which are worth the effort—the coming of the Kingdom among us.

We have suggested that four elements form the "folded structure" of religious life and congregational identities: they are a bridge between the sacred and the secular; a witness to a religiously focused lifestyle; offer a trajectory of becoming holy and finding fullness; and are a witness to what matters—the values of the coming of the Kingdom. Following our analogy of how plants adapt, not only to survive but also to prosper in new environments, we suggest that these elements are among those which can provide the "packing and locking" movements as congregations move toward their future. They serve to stabilize a forward movement and generate new life in changing circumstances. Since all life grows in relationship, our next inquiry will be how the vows of religious life can be understood in secular society as layers of engagement between a religious, God, the church, and the world.

PART II

Toward the Future of Religious Life

4

The Vows in Secular Culture

For many, to take an important step in life is a statement about what life means. They stake their life on their decision. Yet not everyone places such meaning behind their choices. As people today decide what is worth their effort, they encounter diverse interpretations and competing explanations of life. A young doctor volunteers for Doctors Without Borders and gives two years to the people of Sudan. Some people judge her as the best in the profession. Others criticize her for her lack of initiative in setting up a practice and "getting her foot in the door" at the local hospital. Today men and women plan their futures and search for meaning as others have before them. In ancient times, humans relied on the fates to unfold the mystery of birth, life, and death. The fates were known to assign individual destinies to humans which provided a hidden map of meaning throughout their lives. The Judeo-Christian tradition went beyond Greek mythology as their experience of God revealed a God of providence. It discovered a divine love which encompasses not only the meaning of the physical universe in creation but the absolute source of Love which grounds each person's life. For Christians, the meaning of life is not something humans just bestow on themselves.[1] Rather it is a response to the greater Reality of God. The knowledge that one is loved generates freedom to respond in love in return. For Christians, knowing divine love and the love of others prompts the freedom to love God in return and to unify their lives around that love in service to others. Vows in religious life, as

---

[1] Karl Rahner, "The Certainty of Faith," in *The Practice of Faith* (New York: Crossroad, 1983), 32.

we will refer to them, are a positive sacred commitment about love, as are other vows. Vows voice the desire to unite the beginnings of love to action and choice over time which will express it, deepen it, and respond to its presence. The vows are more than a means to an end. Religious are unlikely to state that the vows explain their lives. Rather, vows express a framework for the self-gift and response to the call of the gospel which will frame their lives over time. The only suitable response to being loved is a self-gift. Through vows, religious—as all those in love, situated in time and the uncertainties of life—take up their lives, give themselves away, and commit their whole person and their future to the love of God and service of God's people.

No lifestyle insures authenticity in this pursuit. Marriage vows echo the elements of all love's beginnings and the intention to seek lifelong love. "For better or worse, richer or poorer, in sickness and in health until death do us part." Inherent to seeking and responding to a great love is relinquishing choosing otherwise. The intention to unite one's freedom and action to do all one can to foster love is the reason for the vow. All vows contain a certain paradox of freedom. The very exercise of freedom brings limits to other choices. To marry Teresa is not to marry Joan. To be free to pursue one good, one must turn from others, or enter them only to the degree they serve the one good. The modern adage, "I want it all" is attractive; however, for one who loves, the happiness of all comes with making choices for some. Keeping a commitment to love engages the whole of life. All the goods sought over a lifetime are touched by this irrevocable choice.[2] Where we live, how we spend our time, what motivates us to continue through difficulties are matters explained by "this one thing necessary." A person with religious vows is not excused from the life choices facing all adults: use of one's gifts, ability to function in the world of work, capacity to relate to others, the potential to develop friendships, and the challenge to face life's ordinariness, boredom, and routine. However, their primary commitment to God and God's people impacts all other pursuits. Former Jesuit Superior General Pedro Arrupe S.J. captures what the ancients testify—yet

---

[2]This term is found in the exercises of St. Ignatius, *The Spiritual Exercises of St. Ignatius*, trans. Louis Puhl. S.J. (Chicago, IL: Loyola Press, 1968).

states it in modern form: "Nothing is more practical than finding God, that is, than falling in love in a quite absolute final way."[3]

In the Christian life, a total response to one's baptism is the ideal of discipleship in all vocations. What is important is not so much the state of life than one's openness to God and God's call to one's own path. The readiness to do God's will manifests itself in every adult lifestyle, unique to each vocation. Theologian Bernard Lonergan adds to this picture details of what following a life path entails. While society has resources to outline a career or financial path, a lifepath has a qualitative dimension to it. Lonergan indicates that people who really desire truth and value in their lives travel three roads which carry them on a path where, on each road, they will change and grow in authentic living. This involves continual movement from an established horizon to a new horizon of knowing, valuing, and acting through passages of intellectual, moral, affective, and religious conversion. In this chapter we will examine the meaning of a vow and its place in the overall framework of an adult Christian life. We will indicate how changes in understanding the Christian life and the relationship between the church and the world impact its understanding today. Lastly, we will note how the three vows of poverty, celibate chastity, and obedience engage the adult journey of authenticity amid secular culture. We hope to show that being a person for God means being one who is for the world and ready to serve others. The vows of religious life are not a path "apart from the world;" at the same time, a primary "attunement to and capacity for God" is characteristic of their unfolding.

The Search for Fullness

Charles Taylor explains that the secular age is not necessarily an irreligious period of history, but a time when the conditions of coming to belief have drastically changed. In contrast to a former age, when it was difficult not to believe in God, people come to belief in a climate where belief in God is one option among others to explain the integrity of life. There have always been rival theories

---

[3]As quoted in Kevin Burke, "Love Will Decide Everything: Pedro Arrupe Recovered the Ignatian 'Mysticism of Open Eyes,'" *America*, November 12, 2007.

about the existence of God and the meaning of life.[4] Yet the situation today is that people live side-by-side with quite different experiences of the same life. Diverse kinds of life experiences foster understanding life in one way or the other and ultimately impact what it is like to live as a believer or an unbeliever.[5] This secular framework is the realm in which the meaning and importance of a vow is understood or unappreciated.

All people share a search for happiness. Taylor calls this a search for "fullness:" a condition which is fuller, richer, and meaningful, more as it "ought to be." People also experience the opposite: a sense of exile or alienation from the condition which they seek and a powerlessness to reach it. Everyday language betrays these states. We hear, "I'm in a good space," or a "bad space." However, most of the time people live their day-to-day lives in a middle condition where they manage to escape the pains of "exile" through routine, contentment, or meaningful aspects of their lifestyle, even though they know they have not reached fullness. Knowing there is more gives one's middle position meaning and purpose.

Jungian analyst Ann Belford Ulanov refers to a similar search in clinical work as the search for a "greater reality."[6] In therapeutic work people seek a "greater reality" within their lives. The long work of spiritual practice seeks the same goal—an experience of wholeness not known before. In the language of mysticism, movement through passages of clarity and fulfillment brings a deeper unification of our inner self. Not only are its fragments knit together in this journey, but we are touched by our primary source.[7] This wholeness cannot be purchased through a self-help tape or achieved through a yoga practice, rather it is the work of a lifetime. Spiritual traditions remind us we are never whole. At the same time, they promise that, even in our broken yet healed condition, we are found by something bigger, more complete, and Whole. It is the

---

[4]St. Augustine remarks that there were 288 interpretations of right living in his time. See: Augustine of Hippo, *The City of God*, trans. Marcus Dodds (New York: Random House, 1950), Book XIX, 1, 669. Here Augustine quotes Marcus Varro.
[5]Charles Taylor, *A Secular Age* (Cambridge, MA: The Belknap Press of Harvard University Press, 2007), 5.
[6]Ann Belford Ulanov, *Spiritual Aspects of Clinical Work* (Einsiedeln: Daimon Verlag, 2004), 225ff, 15ff.
[7]Ibid., 19.

Whole and we are the parts. In the Christian life, the Wholeness of God establishes God's life in us and keeps us whole, even when we are broken. The Spirit affirms in us, not that we are already whole, but that the Whole summons us to construct whole living on earth as part of our own journey. To do this, we must venture beyond the security of our now, and risk encounter with the unknown in its many manifestations in life.

The account of the human journey given so far sets the stage for understanding the vows and religious life as an engagement in mystery, yet a commitment to an ordinary life. Speaking of contemporary religious life, Kevin Dowling CSsR. comments on this aspect: "With the developments at Vatican II and afterwards, the theology of baptism and the promotion of the universal call to holiness and so forth, there had to be a re-visioning of the fundamental call and meaning of the religious life."[8] The vows could no longer be understood as a set of norms and ascetical practices in view of achieving a state of holiness or perfection. Their meaning must go beyond depicting a set of "brakes" on life. The *Catechism of the Catholic Church* describes the "evangelical counsels" as "having as their goal the removal of anything which . . . could be an obstacle to the development of charity" (no. 1973). In this passage, the vows are depicted in the classical apophatic tradition as a way of emptying, or selflessness—a step toward self-creating.[9] The vows, though, are more than brakes. They are heartfelt expressions of a gift of self as love for God and God's people. Their primary value is not in what they remove, but in what they foster: the deep, personal commitment to love of God and neighbor. In all, the path of religious life engages the whole of life, including that within us which is "on the way," and gets in the way of this deeper fulfillment. In practice, religious life involves the challenges of beginning an adult life, working through the issues of its middle passage, and facing the journey of aging which all share in the church.

---

[8]Kevin Dowling, CSsR., "Revisioning Religious Life for the 21st Century in a Global Context," talk given at the Annual General Meeting of the Conference of Religious of Ireland, June 4, 2015. As cited in Maria Cimperman RSCJ, *Religious Life for Our World: Creating Communities of Hope* (Maryknoll, NY: Orbis Books, 2020), note 21, 144.
[9]Mary Frohlich, *Breathed into Wholeness: Catholicity and Life in the Spirit* (New York: Orbis Books, 2019), 147.

Boundaries and Frameworks

Aristotle and Socrates asked long ago: what is a life worth living? This question, asked in many forms over the centuries, involves a vision of the potentials of a human person, the type of actions which express them, and an assessment of what brings fulfillment. Today, the modern person engages with these classical questions in their search to be authentic. The meaning of vows has a place in this search. The vows represent one answer to a good life and how to find it. To measure matters of value requires a yardstick which serves to distinguish between the good and the destructive. One needs to know how to develop the dispositions to become a person who lives a fruitful life. No one pursues life goods without personal relationships which are life-giving, and which call one out of self. All serious relationships require agreement on the conditions in which a good life can be experienced and what is required to create such a life together. No one who has shared an intimate relationship with another has done so without a joint vision around some or all of the above matters. We know that not all marriages or friendships are the same. They differ and have elements which are unique to the people in them. Yet without common agreement they do not last.

A religious community formally addresses common assumptions about a framework of life. While not static—it changes with new conditions and develops over time—it has constants. Neither totally new, nor drawn only from traditions, the persons or people who form their communities sustain its character. It demands personal and group boundaries, which contribute to its sense of identity and direction. A religious congregation expresses the core of this framework in their constitutions and other important statements regarding their ongoing life together. However, it is their lived reality which expresses the "spirit" of their life together. This congregational framework of meaning is an essential setting in which religious live their vows.

Ulanov cautions against the dangers of boundaries which are too rigid or too lax. Boundaries defined too tightly result in splitting off the unacceptable from the acceptable, which often translates into prejudice, exclusion, scapegoating, persecution, and the inability to integrate what is different from that which is familiar.[10] To define the boundaries too loosely leaves us like liquid without a container.[11] Members can feel adrift or wonder how they belong. Rootlessness or zoning out in various forms of alienation arise from no longer being able to locate the ways in which they connect to each other and to others. A sense of belonging is threatened. Communities cannot take steps toward a common future, or tackle problems with goals or plans, if they can no longer agree on what those goals are or how to get there. The feeling that the group has lost its compass can occur. Both for individuals and groups, frameworks are necessary so all can find or create, even during transitions, little bits at a time of true living and authentic expression.[12] In these times, communities must trust the Spirit to bring the fragments of their efforts into the wholeness of the experience of the Kingdom in their lives today.

Finally, not attending to boundaries can cause a loss of hope. There can be a loss of contact with the Energy who draws us forward. If groups do not name for themselves who God is and how God is moving in their lives now, they tend to relate to God anonymously, collectively, in the language of inherited tradition or nostalgia, without ever putting their current relationship with God into personal language in their time in history. The sacrifice of boundaries that once defined self or a congregation which have changed is a form of the emptying and receiving new life of the Spirit today. At the same time, it is necessary to seek to reclaim and articulate the meaning of their life together now in order to ground congregational life in the present and to provide a bridge to the future so others can continue the journey which others have taken before.[13]

[10]Peter Cantwell, "Why Newly Professed Leave," *Review for Religious* 62 (2003): 379–401.
[11]Sociologist Zygmunt Bauman marks the passage from an organized society to a "liquid" society where belongings, as well as identities are never automatically—or once and for all—are assured. Postmodern society often involves constant mobility and change in relationships and identities. See: *Liquid Modernity* (Cambridge: Polity Press, 2000).
[12]Ulanov, *Spiritual Aspects of Clinical Work*, 236–9.
[13]Mary Frohlich comments that characteristic of our times is a cultural tension between a softening and fragmentation of personal identity, along with a tendency to react to outsiders with a hardened boundary or violence. The boundaries of the vows are to form a person free of both approaches of modern life. *Breathed into Wholeness*, 75ff.

The Common Road and
Uncommon Journey

The desire to understand the vows in secular society places us in a challenging situation. Society itself does not have a language for a religiously-grounded vowed commitment, even though people in society live these values today. Within the church, the place of religious life has changed and previous frameworks of meaning are no longer adequate to express their meaning. Among the many issues to be addressed, two key questions might lead a way through this impasse. How is religious life connected to those, open to transcendence in secular society, who live a committed life attending to the good of others and society? How are religious distinct from, yet in common with, the search for holiness which marks all the baptized?

Charles Taylor reminds us that both believer and unbeliever share in the same secular world. A religious must understand the vowed life within a society that tells them this world is all there is. Taylor states it clearly: "Secularity in this sense is a matter of the whole context of understanding in which our moral, spiritual, or religious experience and search takes place."[14] In contrast a sense of calling, to which the vows are a response, implies there is a reality beyond oneself to call. The vows previously relied on a former understanding of how the world works for their understanding. The premodern period connected this world to one where being itself exists on several levels and where the cosmos manifests a hierarchy and order. This was the "common sense" of society. In this construal of the world the cosmos functions as a sign that points beyond itself, to what is more than nature. It testifies to divine purpose and action. Its order and design point to the creator, and order and purpose for all created. The sense of calling in this world order depicted religious life as a "higher calling."

Since premodern times there have been various philosophical shifts in the understanding of the world. Some values of this world remain important in the spiritual life; a sense of a reality beyond the self yet connected to the self remains. Believers still listen for the

---

[14]Ulanov, *Spiritual Aspects of Clinical Work*, 3.

possible self-manifestation of God in their experience and interpret it.[15] Those who are not open to transcendence deny this possibility. They may interpret their experiences as psychological phenomena, as unhappy or happy, positive or tragic. Others may have the same experiences as believers yet hold there is no other dimension impacting their lives. The "more" in life is understood in terms of the potential which human beings can accomplish in the here and now. Unlike the believer they do not experience help from above; the potential to reach "more" is only "within."[16] To make the world better, they can make laws and order the world. They can, with their own efforts, deal with what challenges human flourishing. Some leave open the door for the role of a higher power or transcendent source, even though they do not have a language to identify or express it. These seekers walk with believers and unbelievers, as they look for more.[17]

Religious live side-by-side with those who share the ideals of making the world a better place. They seek human fulfillment and flourishing for themselves and for others. They accept that the meaning of life involves both their own fulfillment and fostering the conditions where others can achieve the same. However, for believers, their faith tells them to look for still more. A sense of calling, as well as the conviction they can have a relationship with God, reflects this deeper search. Awareness of how God is in life is not always clear to a religious as they move through the passages of their lives. This they share with all in the church. Yet their vocation is one which is fit for a lifetime, therefore, the renewal of this search is an ongoing element in it.

So, what is the distinction between religious life and the lives of others of goodwill who share their concerns for the world? Karl Rahner claims we cannot give meaning to ourselves, nor can we prove that our lives have meaning. While at times we ponder our lives in terms of the good and the problems which have entered it, we find a "balance sheet" of good and bad cannot give us an answer. Rather, people must surrender " . . . to the hope of an incalculable

---

[15]Taylor, *A Secular Age*, 25, 43, 161.

[16]Ibid., 9.

[17]Roger Haight, S.J., *Christian Spirituality for Seekers: Reflections on the Spiritual Exercises of Ignatius Loyola* (New York: Orbis Books, 2012).

final reconciliation of their existence, marked by the presence of the One whom we call God."[18] To enter the horizon of viewing my life as a calling, rather than just a series of choices, I must be open to thinking of it in this way to recognize a call. I must posture myself to be addressed. In addition, I must risk the meaning of this call to direct how I live over a lifetime. To receive the gifts of faith, hope, and love necessary to live the two great commandments in religious life, requires this leap of faith.

When we read of the great conversion experiences of the saints, we may realize that our own lives do not have the intensity of the great self-authenticating experiences they have encountered. Their own points of contact with the source of fullness gave them a sense of the heightened power of love itself which God opened for them. However, the conviction that others have been closer to this source than we have is common. It is an essential part of the ordinary person's confidence in a shared religious language. The language one uses to define one's life is given force by the conviction that others have lived it in a more complete, direct, and powerful manner. This is part of what it means to belong to a church and to trust in the trajectories of living the faith that the communion of saints offers us.[19] A person can posture themselves to be addressed because in some way a "community of witnesses" has helped them to do so. This is true over the course of the life of a religious, not just in its initial call. Vows are always carried out through and with the people encountered in life. Without them, the good and the difficult, it is an impossible journey. The communion of saints enters our lives in official and unofficial forms.

Baptism

Christians interpret experiences of being deeply touched and moved by life events as an experience of God. It seems fair to ask why everyone does not give such an interpretation to their life experience. The

---

[18]Karl Rahner, "Experience of the Holy Spirit," in *Theological Investigations*, ed. Edward Quinn, Vol. XVIII (New York: Crossroad, 1963), 200. See also, Merkle, *Beyond Our Lights and Shadows*, 101.
[19]Taylor, *A Secular Age*, 729.

possibility of interpreting a depth to life has the precondition that one has been taught to do so or is open to do so. For some, they do not have a religious background. For others, the societal message, that what occurs on the surface is all there is, is simply accepted. Another group simply cuts themselves off from certain experiences because of skepticism.[20]

Through their baptism, all Christians, married, single, vowed religious or ordained, are to allow their Christian faith to animate and direct their lives. This is their Christian vocation and calling. Vatican II makes it clear that "all the faithful of Christ, of whatever rank or status, are called to the fullness of the Christian life and to the perfection of charity" (LG 40). The Christian life is also a call to ministry—explicit in baptismal commitment. Every baptized person is called to do more than "save their souls:" they are called to love and serve others. Today we recognize that the life of every baptized person should be a visible response to both great commandments. Love the Lord your God with all your heart, with all your strength, with all your mind, and your neighbor as yourself (see: Mt. 22:37-39), even if this is done in ordinary ways.

While Christians share with all the desire to make the world a better place, and see it as an essential part of the Christian life, they know that salvation is irreducible to human actions alone. Christians seek to live constructively with and for others, in the style of the paschal mystery, knowing God is present in their lives. In the words of John Paul II: "The Kingdom of God being in the world without being of the world, throws lights on the order to human society, while the power of grace penetrates that order and gives it life" (CA 25). The call of baptism in the Christian life is the basis of the vows, it distinguishes the meaning of religious life beyond the service it provides, and it attests to union with God as central to human fulfillment in all vocations.

Religious Life

A calling to religious life is understood best as something more than what is necessary, in face of a God who is beyond a requirement in

---

[20]Hans Joas, *Do We Need Religion?* trans. Alex Skinner (London: Paradigm, 2008), 13.

one's life. To understand the nature of the vows requires the logic of superabundance, the sense of gift. The Spirit, who grounds the religious experience of being loved by God, evokes joy—even in knowledge which fluctuates between clarity and unknowing, and lacks words.[21] The joy arises from an awareness of being loved and delighted. While awareness of God's love is possible in the life of every Christian, the vows are a recognition of this love personally which fulfills the religious as a person in a lifelong commitment. Joy is the foundation of the vows, even though the feeling of joy is not a constant in everyday experience. This fundamental dimension of the "yes" of the vows grounds the ups and downs, the dark passages and the successes, the health and the illness, the acceptance, the misunderstandings, and the ordinariness of the life of the religious. For this reason, theologically the vows of a religious are an act of worship. Today this language may seem distant to modern sensibilities, but its roots are not. The vows are an act of worship as they reflect the postures of gratitude, appreciation, and dedication to God.[22]

Aware that our "self" has many dimensions, we might ask, what is a worshipping self? It is not likely to be the first adjective that comes to mind in self-description. The posture of worship is first and foremost an awareness of a greater reality than ourselves. A worshipping self is not an isolated "I;" his or her identity is found in a community, with a narrative, a tradition, and a practice.[23] It is a person who relies on more than self-esteem, who looks for recognition by God as a radical affirmation of self-worth. A worshipping self holds others in esteem and nurtures concern for another's good, as one's own. They are ready to sacrifice for another and for the common good—as the Eucharist celebrates. God's relationship with all creation invites the

---

[21]"The most appropriate way to describe this experience of givenness is to employ a personal metaphor: we perceive the givenness which characterizes infinite mystery as a *personal* appeal which creates a *personal* relationship that begins to fulfill us *as persons.*" Anthony J. Godzieba, *A Theology of the Presence and Absence of God* (Collegeville, MN: Liturgical Press, 2018), 183.
[22]Waldemar Molinski, "Vow," in *Sacramentum Mundi*, ed. Karl Rahner, Vol. 6 (New York: Herder and Herder, 1970), 350–2.
[23]Here I rely on some the sentiments of David Ford in his reflection on the role of worship in the Christian life. See: David F. Ford, *Self and Salvation: Being Transformed* (Cambridge, MA: Cambridge University Press, 2003), 97ff.

worshipping self into the love God has for each as well as concern that the goods of the earth are available for all, and its integrity is respected. The worshipping self—in the many postures of life expressed in prayer: lament, confession of sin, expression of hopes and fears, affirmations of faith, praise, petitions, prophecies, blessings, curses, and moments of wisdom—witnesses to the truth of God in face of all that testifies to God's absence.

The image of the vows as an act of worship points to two aspects of religious life which might elude us. First, religious engage in the life struggles and joys of becoming authentic shared with all and walk the common journey of light and darkness of all believers.[24] Second, religious life is best described through the language of the abundance of the Kingdom, the hundredfold (Mark 10:30), which cannot be captured by any set of rules or calculations alone. The gospel calls for an ethic of generosity which goes beyond a calculation of costs and benefits, as all great loves would testify. While the hundredfold of the Kingdom invites gratitude for all life brings, a closer look at the process of conversion sheds light on some of the concrete passages of the journey. A vow only seals the desire to engage in this journey; insight into the process sheds light on some ways conversion unfolds in practice.

Lonergan and Conversion

The term "conversion," or major alternation in viewpoint or attitude, is a movement from an established horizon to a new horizon of knowing, valuing, and acting which involves intellectual, moral, affective, and religious conversion.[25] Our deepest conversions happen at the level of why we do what we do. One does not follow Jesus in the paschal mystery all at once, but through a process which happens over time. If our deepest conversion happens at the level of why we do what we do, a deeper look at these intersections offers a view of the life of the

---

[24]See: Godzieba, *A Theology of the Presence and Absence of God,* for a development of this aspect of the theology of God in the Christian tradition.
[25]Richard N. Fragomeni, "Conversion," in *The New Dictionary of Catholic Spirituality*, ed. Michael Downey (Collegeville, MN: The Liturgical Press, 1993), 234.

vows over a life course. Conversion leads to human and spiritual integration as well as involves vertical and horizontal dimensions: our relationship with God, with others, and with ourselves. These differences, while seemingly indistinguishable externally in day-to-day life, make conversion in the Christian life distinct from the noble becoming of exclusive humanism. Lonergan's depiction of the nature of intellectual, moral, affective, and religious conversion can point to deeper aspects of this process.

Intellectual

An experience of intellectual conversion is portrayed in the story of Jesus and the two disciples on the road to Emmaus (Lk. 24:13-35). It was difficult for the apostles, who did not recognize Jesus, to imagine this stranger did not know about the events of Jesus' own passion and death. They tell him all. The apostles here are like us, we already know everything and how things are. Jesus' response to them is simple, "What little sense have you." Jesus then explains things to them.

The story shows that the disciples eventually did recognize Jesus and returned to Jerusalem, rather than fleeing from it. They knew Jesus beyond their first impressions, or their second, or their hundredth, and this ongoing experience is the heart of intellectual conversion in the Christian life. We know we are open to intellectual conversion when our encounter with Christ can change our minds about life, about people, and about ourselves in an ongoing way. Intellectual conversion is our capacity to be willing to be open to what is true, what makes sense. Intellectual conversion is tied up ultimately with the heart of what it means to be human.

To engage in this process, we must use our human capacities to experience, understand, and judge many areas of life with the resources available to us. Failure to convert intellectually can come as much from taking the line of least resistance and not exerting the effort to inform ourselves, as well as from gossip and obstinacy. Living in communities challenges a religious to move beyond any group bias which obstructs a common search for truth. Both personally, and as communities, we can fail to convert intellectually because of a natural tendency to bias, to thinking which serves our immediate gratification rather than an understanding which leads to a more accurate picture of what is true and will lead to what is ultimately good.

Moral

Moral conversion is a gradual process by which we do things, not just for the satisfaction it brings us, but because it is the right thing to do. We shift our criteria for decision-making from the satisfaction of the self as the basis of choice, to the discovery and pursuit of value. The Christian life is not just one of avoiding sinful behavior but of cultivating virtue, becoming a new person, and promoting values worth the effort. Understanding moral conversion goes beyond a self-initiated pursuit of perfection often confused with the course of religious life, or the Christian life. Changes in how we understand the dynamics of Christian becoming impact our grasp of moral conversion.

Traditionally, the moral life was focused on all human persons and the universal goals of human becoming. Thomas Aquinas drew attention to the highest goal—that our minds be attached to God. The person was but one member of the human species and, as a rational animal, shared with all human beings common faculties and this same ultimate goal. Human actions had a purpose: human fulfillment—this fulfillment was a type of linear development of human capacities that all people shared.[26] The theologian Hans Urs von Balthasar does not negate the wisdom in Aquinas' understanding, but he also reflects that people today see their life a little differently—more as a narrative, a life story. The contingencies and concrete events of one's life tell a story, and we as humans seek its meaning. The actions of an individual are given purpose by being united by and interpreted within a story that says something true about the person, an inner truth so important that it is constitutive of the person themselves. The person's "truth" gives unity to their lives. We judge past and future actions in light of how they "fit" into a broader life course, or story, which we have begun. We can either enrich this story or deplete it through neglect or rebellion.

---

[26]Christopher Steck, S.J., *The Ethical Thought of Hans Urs von Balthasar* (New York: Crossroad, 2001), 73 ff.

From a theological perspective, the narrative of our identity is not just self-constructed, it is given by God. It involves more than our self-esteem; it is rooted in recognition by the Other. Von Balthasar recognizes the common experience that there is often a gap between one's true identity and how one understands one's story. We often see ourselves worse or better than we are. He reminds us that the human person cannot give themselves the ultimate validity which can only come from God. Their true identity is revealed to them over time in continued encounters with God. Even though, for Aquinas, the highest act or fulfillment of a person is the knowing, willing, and loving the Absolute, for von Balthasar it is becoming a "self" in relation to the Absolute, to relate one's unique "I," one's identity, to the Absolute.[27] Moral conversion is the process by which one continually enters this relationship.

Attention to the process of moral conversion also highlights how religious share in the universal call to holiness in the church as well as the summons to an authentic humanity shared with all people. Norbert Rigali S.J. offers insight into this shared experience. Ethics, that is, where rightness and wrongness of conduct is concerned, has four levels.[28] First there are essential ethics. These include norms that are regarded as applicable to all persons, where one's behavior is an instance of a general, essential moral norm. Rightness and wrongness of acts of killing, keeping promises, not stealing, are included, as well as all actions rooted in the dignity of persons as human beings. The second level, existential ethics, refers to the awareness that "this ought to be done by me." This is a sense of "ought" addressed to the individual: I "ought" to go to that funeral. I "ought" to use my musical talents for others. The third is essential Christian ethics. These are ethical decisions a Christian must make because he or she belongs to a community to which the non-Christian does not belong. To belong to a worshipping community, to educate one's children in the faith, and to attend to the teachings of the church would be included.

The fourth is an existential Christian ethic. These are decisions in a faithful life that carry with them a fuller sense of conversion, which logically might be missing from the other types of moral

---

[27]Ibid., 76.
[28]Norbert Rigali, S.J., "On Christian Ethics," *Chicago Studies* 10 (1971): 227–47.

calls. These decisions often go beyond the moment. It could be a call to follow a religious vocation, to accept responsibility in the community, to care for someone with special needs, or to adopt a child. What marks a Christian ethic is not just a difference in motivation on the part of the Christian. It is the posture that what I do, I do in union with Christ. This difference can evoke a different response of content.

This fourth type of Christian ethics rests on the assumption that the Christian response to Christ in love in not simply one-dimensional: we love Christ but also Christ loves us. Von Balthasar brings this posture into his whole sense of morality, it involves a twofold movement whereby we receive Christ's love and then we act.[29] He draws on St. Ignatius of Loyola, who states that we are created first to praise, revere, and serve God, and all things are to be ordered to this first calling.[30] To accept this call, we surrender to God and then make choices. This is quite different from the self-realization of the autonomous person, the buffered self. Instead, there is a giving of self to God and a reception of self from God. The person asks, how does this decision look to God's eyes, not simply the God of the commandments, but God who loves me and calls me to my true identity?

This is the twofold movement of interpersonal love. Christ moves toward me, a creature, in self-emptying, and the human being reaches toward God. Here the person allows himself or herself to be *changed* by this encounter, and to allow emotions, ideas, plans, and strategies to be altered by what one learns in this personal exchange. Rahner indicates that mysticism is not just for unusual people; everyday mysticism and von Balthasar's explanation earlier both affirm that this is not an encounter for spiritual specialists alone. It is the model for the daily life of Christians in postmodern society. The paschal mystery lies at the heart of the Christian life. George Aschenbrenner reminds us, "The challenge facing us Christians is surely not to raise ourselves . . . Rather our challenge is to learn, in everyday situations . . . a life not centered on ourselves, but

---

[29]Steck, *The Ethical Thought of Hans Urs von Balthasar*, 77–9.
[30]Tim Muldoon, "Postmodern Spirituality and the Ignatian *Fundamentum*," *The Way* 44, no. 1 (January 2005): 88–100.

heartily engaged in a personal, real relationship with our consoling Companion whose faithfulness is beyond doubt."[31]

This vision of moral conversion in the life of the vows involves a "freedom from" and a "freedom to." Human fulfillment in postmodern life involves several challenges: the desire to overcome the meaninglessness associated with the contingency of human life, to achieve a personal identity grounded in the absolute, and the desire to gain self-possession through interpersonal love. These aspects of the Christian life in secular times impact an understanding of indifference. Indifference, as a marker of the Christian life, is not just a moving away from things of the world, often associated with religious life. An indifference which grows out of a dynamic relationship with God moves back and forth: from an initial detachment regarding earthy goods, toward a reengagement of those goods, now with desires and love attuned to those of God, and God's desires for the Kingdom in the lives of others.[32] The role of religious in taking responsibility for the world enters this vision. Indifference enables something new to happen. Black theologian James Cone says if you want to witness the transcendent in modern society, you better do something different than business as usual.[33] Political theologians echo Cone's sentiment in referring to a "break" or a "discontinuity" which goes beyond just a doing or an activity. It is an action of true freedom as it imitates the love of Jesus in the concrete realities of one's social existence. Such action requires a type of indifference to what is self-serving. The Christian life gives rise to an inherent paradox which impacts the practice of the vows. Autonomy and initiative understood through the Christian mysteries lead to an increasing dependence on God. Dependence on God fosters a deeper and more radical autonomy and initiative. Yet, knowing God as one's supreme good is not the same as knowing what to do in a concrete situation. Religious by vow are also called communities to contribute to the critical reason needed in their societies. The encyclicals written by the recent popes

---

[31]George Aschenbrenner, "A Consoling Companion, Faithful Beyond Any Doubt," *The Way* 46, no. 3 (July 2007): 67–83.
[32]Steck, *The Ethical Thought of Hans Urs von Balthasar*, 79.
[33]James Cone, *Speaking the Truth: Ecumenism, Liberation and Black Theology* (Grand Rapids, MI: Eerdmans, 1986), 118.

to the church and to the world remind us that the future promised by God often cannot be conceived adequately under the conditions of the present. Conversion of heart and mind is needed. It is here that we meet the intersection of intellectual and moral conversion in the ongoing journey of faithfulness.

Religious

Religious conversion is the love of God. On an experience level, it is an interior change whereby our ordinary cares are placed in this larger context of transcendent meaning and value. Religious conversion is the actual broadening of our own personal perspectives, from focusing only on the realities of our finite world, to attending to matters of ultimate meaning and value as well. It orients us to the whole and to a valuing of each person and event in themselves and in the ultimate significance they have. Religious conversion grounds us in the "more" of hope, a "more" of love" in our attitude and actions. It is not blind to the complexities, problems, and ambiguities of human existence. Rather, to the degree it is alert to the larger and more beneficent meaning of reality, it can face evil with courage because it does not fear that evil will have the last word. It reflects this eschatological perspective. Religious conversion witnesses that the love of God produces a dynamic state of being in love; that the grace of God that communicates divine life becomes the inmost definer of what the religious person is. Openness to religious conversion and desire for it allows the love of God to assist the full ripening of our own authenticity.[34] This does not happen all at once, but in stages throughout the lifecycle.

Religious conversion as a process is fostered by simplicity of heart. Simplicity, the heart of religious conversion, helps us to know not only God's love but our incapacity for sustained spiritual development apart from God's ongoing redeeming love for us. Ideas of religious life as a "higher state" implying a "higher" character than those in other situations is mistaken. Without the gift of simplicity, we dodge the need to "know ourselves," which is key to ongoing conversion. We may immerse ourselves in worthwhile activities,

---

[34]See: *The Desires of the Human Heart: An Introduction to the Theology of Bernard Lonergan.* ed. Vernon Gregson (New York: Paulist Press, 1988), 57 ff., 92ff.

but we refuse to be open to an ongoing awareness of the impact of our own words, actions, and mixed motives on ourselves and others. We may mete out our praise and blame to others, and simply ignore any assessments of ourselves.[35] We can easily rationalize our moral responsibilities—either by denying them or enlarging them to salvific proportions. Most significant, we can easily give up hope, and no longer meet the challenges it implies.

It is one thing to observe a decline in numbers in religious life, it is another to enter a dynamic of decline, either personally or in the groups to which we belong. In a decline which is more serious than a numerical one, we lose sight of the Risen Christ active in our history and our daily lives individually and as a group, and stop trying. Openness to conversion requires remaining in the tension in life between limitation and transcendence.[36] When we lose balance held by limitations of our moment in time, we can displace this energy in anger and depression, no longer able to witness hope for others for the future. We can overstate our capacities and be caught in frenetic activity. Simplicity opens us to the grace of ongoing conversion in our lives as it is the priority of the heart of the gospel that focuses us on God. The life of the vows continually requires a turning to simplicity for reorientation and focus.

Affective

To some degree affective conversion is indistinguishable from religious conversion. Affective conversion is the transformation of desire. It is a move from selfish desire to generosity, from the possessiveness rooted in obsessive concern for one's own needs to the self-giving of generative love of others. It is the move from duty to passionate commitment. It is the reorientation of our motivations, not just our behavior.

Deep within us is the capacity to transcend ourselves, to go out of ourselves in love rather than into ourselves in egotism. When a person falls in love, that love is expressed not just in this act or that

---

[35]Bernard J. Lonergan, *Insight* (San Francisco, CA: Harper and Row, 1978), 599.
[36]Robert Doran, "From Psychic Conversion to the Dialectic of Community," in *Lonergan Workshop*, Vol. 6, ed. Robert C. Croken, Frederick F. Crowe, and Robert M. Doran, S.J. (Toronto: University of Toronto Press, 1990), 84.

act, but in a dynamic state of being in love. Today this is a good image for being in the state of grace. Being in love is the center from which all else flows—one's desires and fears, one's joys and sorrows, one's discernment of values, one's decisions and needs.[37] Such falling in love is a radical transformation in a person's life; life is never the same. Yet expressing that love in daily life requires the grace of one's vocation. Gradually, there is a shift from one's interests alone to a concern for the good of others.

If in moral conversion we see the possibility which is open to us to do the right thing and feel its challenge, because through intellectual conversion we opened our mind to new possibilities, in affective conversion we take the next step. In affective conversion we find the power to make an effective response and execute that decision over the long haul and against serious obstacles. Affective conversion takes us beyond duty. If we reflect on Mary, the mother of Jesus, I do not think we see her dutifully taking care of Jesus. She carried in her heart the whole posture of the Christian life, a deep and sustaining love of God which held nothing back. Here the emotion of love is more than a feeling of psychological origin. Rosemary Haughton's *Passionate God* holds that we can make sense of how God loves us by looking at the way people love, particularly the way of love called passionate. By "passionate" she means to evoke something—to put something in motion, strong, wanting, needy, concentrated toward a very deep encounter.[38] She goes on to say we can recognize a value so strongly that the response to it transforms vague longing into intense passions. It can engage us totally. But the same recognition can be so profound that it can seem like a void or a gap. Passion is the thrust which leaps that void without guarantee or even knowledge: it is a leap of faith. In this passionate love, lovers come to self-awareness in the awareness of the beloved; they are defined in the very exchange of life that is love. It is the deep love that sustains us over a life course, even when its initial fervor is not felt.

This realization returns us to religious conversion. For Lonergan, the question of God and ultimate transcendence flows from our

---

[37]Bernard J. Lonergan S.J., *Method in Theology* (Toronto: University of Toronto Press, 1990), 105.
[38]Rosemary Haughton, *The Passionate God* (New York: Paulist, 1981), 6.

core capacities as human beings to experience, understand, judge, and decide. When we respond to the possibilities of life, our "radical intending," we do so through these capacities. They are the ground or means by which we pursue specific questions, projects, and life decisions. They are the way we continually seek the intelligible, the true, and the good. In religious life, these pursuits make concrete the more intangible intentions of our heart, expressed in the self-gift of the vows. In Karl Rahner's terms, they are the categorical (concrete) expressions of our transcendental (posture toward what is Absolute) intentions. They are the way we express what is in our hearts and the kind of person we want to be.

Unless the human spirit is truncated, it spontaneously will ask about the whole, the ground, the origin of itself and the world, or the question of God. It will ask, what is it all about, meaning life itself? God, therefore, is part of human authenticity because what is human by nature requires constant self-transcendence or unfurling. It involves the constant struggle not to let narrower capacities define our meaning and the meanings of our communities. God also is the ultimate basis of all our loves, in friendship, in marriage, in religious life, and in church and society. These loves actualize our capacities for self-transcendence and point to its ultimate source: God's love, which is God's own doing. The God of biblical faith is the God of mystery who can change our lives. Hence the love by which we respond to God in religious conversion is unrestricted; it sets up a new horizon. While it is impossible to separate the love that expresses religious vows from other loves, which establish commitments over a lifetime, Lonergan's framework can suggest ways we can lean toward a distinction which might serve as a means of clarification. The former language of higher and lower vocations of single, married, and religious vocations is not helpful. Another path of distinction might serve to identify the grace of these different callings and their mystery and, within this wider picture, encompass our focus on religious life.

The Vows

Religious experience is not something that we can know or understand as we can know or understand other experiences, working out their meanings and realities through the processes of being attentive to experience, understanding, and judging. Rather than these prior three levels of our consciousness, religious experience is the fourth level of consciousness: of choosing and loving what we have sought through these other modes of being human. Here one makes judgments of value in contrast to judgments of the truth of meaning which characterize the third level of judgment. The pursuit of what is of ultimate value fulfills all the intentional desires the person sought consciously at the other levels.

There is a difference between the self-consistency we seek between knowing and doing on the third level of consciousness— trying to be informed and make good decisions—and the decision which stems from religious conversion, the fourth level. While all involve the grace of God, the one stemming from a religious conversion is of an unrestricted orientation. We seek to "know and do, not just what pleases us, but what is truly good, worthwhile," and so to "be principles of benevolence and beneficence, capable of genuine collaboration and of true love."[39]

This is being in love in an unrestricted manner. At this level, we share in the divine nature in the deepest way. In the choice to make religious vows, I recognize that this expression of relationship is part of who I am at the deepest level. Mark 12:30 tells us we can love God with our whole heart, with our whole soul, with our whole mind, and with our whole strength. The Epistle to the Romans states that hope does not disappoint because God's love has been poured into our hearts through the Holy Spirit (Rom. 5.5). The experience at this fourth level of consciousness is that through grace we are capable of God, and we trust this grace in our response to what we identify as a call to do so. The distinction of religious life is the directness of this response.

Poverty is a symbolic expression; we have set our hopes for fulfillment and security not on material possessions only but on the richness of the kingdom. In these times of transition of religious life we experience this at a new level. Our hope is not in our institutions, the numbers in our novitiates, or the power of our place in the church as we search for the next steps for our congregations. We trust that God will lead us on the path God has

---

[39]Lonergan, *Method in Theology*, 35. See also, Robert Doran, "Discernment and Lonergan's Fourth Level of Consciousness," *Gregorianum* 89, no. 4 (2008): 790–802.

for us. The commitment of voluntary celibacy is a statement that my passionate love of God is as concrete as the setting aside of the definite loves of husband, wife, and family and its energy will be sustained and my becoming will be marked with a hundredfold of relationships which encompass a full life. The vow of obedience is a tangible way of expressing that the active presence of Jesus is in the community, the church, and the real people with whom I will collaborate. It is a manifestation of confidence that the work of the kingdom will come through the "earthenware vessels" of real people and structures, with those who hold authority, and those with whom I will journey.

Lonergan's explanation of the consequences of religious conversion contributes to the understanding of the whole of religious life. The transformation of the person is co-extensive with the animation of community at a familial, social, cultural, ecclesial, and global level. Religious life is not just a choice for the individual. To the degree that individuals and groups are willing to walk the path of human and spiritual conversion there exists the possibility of the transformation of all the areas of human life which block the human drive toward authentic living. The possibility that human dignity, ecological integrity, international peace, civic security, racial equality, gender equity, family integrity, and nonviolence can exist and characterize our civilization is tied to the willingness to overcome what deters them. Conversion on a personal level involves the challenge to the ideologies and patterns of conduct which maintain all these systems which inhibit human flourishing. Different from an approach to these issues at the level of society alone, the mentality of exclusive humanism, is the awareness in the Christian life there is something more than human flourishing. Religious combine their work for justice and their commitment to evangelization. To the degree that our societies define this flourishing often around economic values and prestige, the vowed life models in a distinct way that there is something more. The vows of religious life mark a style of living the Christian life which testifies to the hope which comes from the gospel in its own way. It grounds the goal of all the baptized to live fully their call and it supports the investment of all those of goodwill who sacrifice for the good of their neighbor and the world.

5

Adult Christian Living in Secular Culture

Vulnerability marks religious congregations today, as religious consider their futures. Concern regarding fewer new members, diminishing financial resources, and a lack of knowledge of new generations, fuels a sense of exposure to forces not considered in the past. These observable concerns are joined by the impact of wider cultural dynamisms. Recognition that people imagine a fulfilled life unbothered by an apparent absence of religious meaning gives rise to the questions, where do we fit? Which way is ahead? For some, the solution is to dismantle the institutional structures under which religious have been operating. To others this seems impossible, fruitless, and destructive. The programmatic alone seems insufficient to sense where the spirit is leading congregations currently. Superficial thinking and fixer-upper solutions hold little promise of success. It may be tempting to dream of an unchartered future, unconnected to the present, yet experience confirms that what emerges is related in some manner to what precedes it. The search for the next step stirs hope in face of the ambiguity which surrounds it. As the church and religious themselves seek direction in new times neither can deny the impact of secular experience and expectations. The path forward involves acceptance of the reality that the church's relevance among its members and in the society at large involves dialogue with secular realities. A consolation is that the church and religious life do not exist in a world apart from secular life. In this chapter we will ask how dialogue with secular realities impacts the adaptations needed by religious as they move into the future.

The dilemma facing religious congregations shares in a wider challenge in first-world societies.[1] Disconnect affects every adult lifestyle in church and society as a new state of the world has emerged. A combination of social, economic, and political forces has joined with changed technology, ideology, and changes in culture to shift society's equilibrium. These elements do not match as we once assumed. A sense of fragmentation both surprises and is commonplace. Social and ethical systems no longer control our technology; our identities as people are no longer defined by the same boundaries; and time-held ideas no longer carry meaning, nor provide the same level of insight into solutions to problems. People and nations jostle for identity and position in the world of shifting ground, often by means which challenge the fabric of our families, communities, and church. The presence and persistence of an international pandemic has simply highlighted the vulnerability of our global systems and ways of proceeding.

While we will ask how these uncertainties affect the future of religious congregations, we acknowledge they also impact married life. Theologian Don Browning charges that, while processes of modernization and globalization provide new possibilities for the prosperity and health of the modern family, they are also a threat to the stability and quality of marriage and family life.[2] Christianity transformed family relations in antiquity. However, families today are disrupted by divorce, out-of-wedlock births, the emerging culture of non-marriage, and the increasing absence of fathers from their children. The collapse of marriage is also a contributing factor to world poverty.[3] Lisa Sowle Cahill recognizes these conditions also challenge a new generation of married Christians: gender equality, more economic stress, consumerism, and in many cases a first-world culture unwilling to deliver justice for all.[4]

[1]Charles Taylor, *The Ethics of Authenticity* (Cambridge, MA: Harvard University Press, 1991), 1–12. See also:
[2]Don S. Browning, *Marriage and Modernization: How Globalization Threatens Marriage and What To Do About It* (Grand Rapids, MI: Eerdmans, 2003), 75.
[3]Ibid., 17, 277.
[4]Lisa Sowle Cahill, "Notes on Moral Theology: Marriage: Developments in Catholic Theology and Ethics," *Theological Studies* 64 (2003): 97. See also: Julie Hanlon Rubio, *Family Ethics: Practices for Christians* (Washington, DC: Georgetown University Press, 2010).

Recently Bertrand Dumas points to how postmodern "spectacularization" threatens Christian marriage. Modern society offers a superficial grasp of marriage and relationships. To feel alive, the postmodern individual seeks the new, the boundary-breaking, and the notable. An increased need for intensity and visibility presents marriage in a false light and obscures its process. The mystery of the love of a marriage is made into the spectacular, and the ordinary is lost in the attempt to make it conform to the remarkable. This mentality feeds a consumer approach to marriage which makes it just another "experience to be enjoyed and then set aside in the search for maximizing the potential for happiness."[5] Apart from the institutions and societal patterns which grounded marriage, a couple is charged to maintain a constant feeling of love through new experiences, in face of the blunt ordinariness of everyday life, which impacts all vocations. The challenge for a theology of marriage is to find mystery in the ordinary, to discover the grace-bestowing power of the sacrament in everyday life experiences. The search for the new, the different, and the improved also is a source of the destabilization of marriage, as a 50 percent divorce rate in many first-world countries indicates. When one or both spouses tire of the other, of the daily routine or the lack of excitement, a theology of marriage needs to support them. "A theology of marriage that does not make central in its reflection boredom as well as desire, being stuck in a routine as well as moments of novelty, weariness as well as hope, stress as well as joy, risks anchoring people in an unrealistic vision of marriage."[6]

The Challenge of Institutions

Religious life, marriage, and life in the church share a common dilemma. All have an institutional element. People in general do not like institutions. Institutions are seen as something from the past, filled with unexamined customs and codes which no longer

---

[5]Bertrand Dumas, "The Sacrament of Marriage in Postmodernity: Struggling with 'Spectacularization,'" *Marriage, Families, and Spirituality* 27, no. 2 (2021): 175–95, at 184.
[6]Ibid., 187.

fit modern society. People find them oppressive. The limitations institutions place on them are judged to be not worth the benefits they provide. Institutions do limit free choice, especially if autonomy is one's highest value. However, many moderns take the benefits of institutions for granted, without taking into account the investments required to provide these important stabilizers in life.

Anthropologist Mary Douglas finds that the situation today is that people need institutions yet feel ambivalent about them. She maintains that people mature through two dominant life patterns which offer different forms of social control. In the first, individuals see themselves in relationship to a structure: that is, hierarchy, sex role, and seniority or age status among others, all enter into self-understanding. Habit and ritual contribute to a coherent symbol system and organized way of life. In the second system, self-understanding is rooted more in the sense of self as an individual. Here control comes through becoming more sensitive to the feelings of others, as one becomes aware of one's feelings. One is influenced by the need for relationship, community, and communion with others; the second by the impetus for authenticity. These two dimensions of living employ two different kinds of language. The first, a condensed code, is institutionally rooted. When a child is told to pick up her toys and asks why, a parent answers in this language, "because I said so." The second occurs when the parent takes another approach and remarks, "How do you think Mom will feel when she comes home, and this place is a mess?" This reflects an elaborated code, one that relies on sensitivity to others. As we mature, elaborated codes, our personal assessments, are used to criticize institutions. However, elaborated codes can never float entirely free of institutions, for we take them for granted as the very basis from which criticism is possible.[7] If people tried to live their lives through elaborated codes alone, they would have to make up their lives as they go along. Nothing could be taken for granted, because there would be no institutional context to tell them where they are. Even our most intimate relationships have an institutional dimension.

---

[7]Mary Douglas, *Natural Symbols: Explorations in Cosmology* (New York: Pantheon Books, 1982), 24, 26.

Both marriage and religious life in secular contexts have relied less on institutional contexts and more on freely consented to and negotiated attachments. Values of freedom, equality, and fulfillment have benefited and softened rigid roles and boundaries in both vocations. But they have also raised expectations regarding how happiness is measured, and the adaptations needed to hold a marriage and a congregation together. In marriage, "For each couple, it is now a matter of combining the plasticity of roles (sexual and parental) with the loss of inherited models, the demand for personal autonomy and the desire for harmony, the daily reiteration of love and lengthening of the life span, emotional investment and the professional advancement of both persons, etc."[8] In congregations, the absence of an internally coherent group spirituality, the conflicting life perspectives of generations, the tension between personal autonomy and group identity, the shift from common or singular professional identities, the needs of the extended lifespan of members, and the range of postures toward the relevance of the church escalate the challenge of how to "hold it all together."

Spiritual Hungers of the Modern Age

Robert Bellah finds that modern religion also possesses a lack of balance between the institutionally rooted and relationally focused languages in its practice. In his study of religion and individualism in American life, *Habits of the Heart*, religion for one woman named Shelia was called Sheilaism. Shelia saw herself as her central "ultimate concern." Bellah remarks, "Sheilaism is rooted in the effort to transform external authority into internal meaning."[9] Religion shifts to being a cosmic selfhood, which magnifies the self to the point that it becomes identified with the world. This allows one to be religious while at the same time transcend family, ethnic culture, and formal religion to define a self—free of external constraint. The illusion is that, free from organized religion, one is not impacted by wider culture, the market, the state, the internet,

---

[8]Dumas, "The Sacrament of Marriage in Postmodernity," 177.
[9]Robert Bellah, *Habits of the Heart: Individualism and Commitment in American Life* (Berkeley, CA: University of California Press, 1985), 235.

social media, etc. The mistake is to deny how all these influences continue to order one's life. Religion as a celebration of self, or religion as eternal authority and regulation, are two caricatures of religion today. Neither form of religion answers the spiritual hunger of the modern age.

The Christian way of life is a way of life in which others are essential; this is a cardinal direction for adaptation for religious. Others are radically essential because life "in Christ," to use theological language, is that of the body, the body of reconciled humankind vivified by the Spirit of the living God.[10] Faith is not a personal reality which one constructs. Rather faith is lived in a tradition, a history of relationships, in an institution in a religious form. As institutional, it is doctrinal moral, ritual, and so on. It is obvious that there is a value in the personal construction of religious identity and its implied elaborated code. The document on religious freedom of Vatican II expresses that no one should be coerced into a religious posture (DH 14). However, it is not accurate to imagine religious belief as a choice between the condensed code of religion and its commitments and the elaborated code of personal faith. Rather, the two are interdependent in the mature Christian.[11]

Religious through the centuries came to religious life because they sensed there were goals in life which could engage a person more fully and completely than simply to survive, prosper, and uncritically live out cultural norms. The spiritual hungers of their own age formed one impetus which led them to a religious congregation. One way to discern how the Spirit is leading religious congregations into the future is to ask how religious life can respond to spiritual hungers today. These broader questions in the culture impact the future of religious congregations because they involve more than changing the "hearts and minds" of individuals to enter religious life. They are questions which also require institutional response. Whatever adult frameworks are adopted in religious life in the future will need to adequately support both members and meet the deepest needs of the age. An individual lifestyle is hard to

---

[10]J. M. R. Tillard, *Flesh of the Church, Flesh of Christ: At the Source of the Ecclesiology of Communion* (Collegeville, MN: The Liturgical Press, 2001), 11–12.
[11]Juan Alfaro, "Faith," in *Sacramentum Mundi*, Vol. 2, ed. Karl Rahner (London: Burns and Oates, 1968), 313.

sustain against the grain, no matter how lofty one's ideals. All adult lifestyles need institutional support. The transformation of religious congregations therefore must meet the needs of a new generation.

Enduring Questions of the Modern Age

Charles Taylor claims that three spiritual hungers pose "enduring questions" facing secular society. They are (1) a desire to separate ourselves from evil and chaos and to anchor in the good; (2) a need to link ordinary life and higher time in a search for meaning; (3) a drive to establish points of contact with fullness/transcendence which makes sense in secular times.[12] He claims these are enduring and unanswered questions because they emerge from the very structures of modern life. It is not the case that these questions were not present in past generations, but the structures of society were in a different relation to them.[13] Inversely, while modern life provides avenues of human flourishing not possible in the past, its synthesis leaves deep human questions without resources. The questions symbolize gaps in meaning which arise from the very way we live today. In the following, we will pose each question and indicate the resources available for response by a religious congregation.

Religious congregations face similar issues as the church at large, as well as comparable conditions to respond. Some in modern culture are open to transcendence, while others are closed. Likely members of a congregation encounter differences regarding faith and belief among family and friends, while sharing similar goals around public issues. This is the experience of "cross pressures" in religious experience today: an explosion of ethical, religious, and atheistic options which surround us with explanations of a

---

[12]Judith A. Merkle, *Discipleship, Secularity and the Modern Self* (London: Bloomsbury/T&T Clark, 2020), 211.

[13]Taylor puts it this way, "We have moved from an era in which religious life was more 'embodied' . . . into one which is more 'in the mind': where the link with God passes more through our endorsing contested interpretations—for instance, of our political identity as religiously defined, or of God as the authority and moral source underpinning our ethical life." Charles Taylor, *A Secular Age* (Cambridge, MA: The Belknap Press of Harvard University Press, 2007), 553–4.

meaningful life.[14] Religious life brings to common questions its own
contribution, yet it must realize its interaction is not a monologue.
It is not the case that religious belief and humanism must argue the
case, and that whoever comes up with the best answer to life's
problems wins. Rather, exclusive humanism and Christian
humanism are both fragile before the questions of modernity.
Neither has a single expression; both contain plural responses
within their respective traditions. Both perspectives will likely
exist within cross pressures, with the reality of the opposing view
challenging their perspective.

It is important to note, however, that Catholic identity in this
process offers content.[15] Catholic identity is a hybrid of modern
sensibility plus an interpretative framework and committed practice
which arises from the content of membership. In this light, church
membership does offer substance to engagement in secular life in
dealing with these enduring questions. Richard McBrien identifies
that Catholic life has its own identifiable characteristics: mediation,
sacramentality, and communion. These characteristics are a unique
resource in the mix with more broadly-held values of human dignity
and responsible relationships that indicate and impact discipleship
and church witness in secular society today.[16] What follows will
comment on the spiritual hungers in modern life, and then identify
how elements of ecclesial and religious life and interpretation of
congregational charism can aid a response. Hopefully this thought
experiment will offer insight to a religious congregation which can
help them sense the Spirit within their unique contexts.

---

[14]Merkle, *Discipleship, Secularity and the Modern Self*, 105.
[15]Catholic identity is essential to the identity of religious congregations. An
"unattached" religious identity not centered in a Christian communion is like
a Christian ethic in name only. A Christian ethic arises from the practice of an
embodied faith community and is fed by it. The challenge to religious congregations
is to articulate their congregational identity within Catholic identity and their
charism in a way that does not reduce it to a personal religious quest alone nor
an identification solely with the institutional frameworks of the past. Rather its
congregational identity must be a *gestalt* of corresponding features of religious life.
See: Patricia Wittberg, "Developing as Institutionally–Based Virtuoso Spirituality,"
271 ff in *From Piety to Professionalism and Back? Transformations of Organized
Religious Virtuosity* (Lanham, MD: Lexington Books, 2006).
[16]We will only comment on how some aspects of church identity are in dialogue with
these questions, not accounting for a full ecclesiology of the church.

A Desire to Separate from Evil and Do Good: Communion and Community

The modern hunger for meaning involves the concrete need to give an answer to evil and suffering. The question of theodicy, how can a good God allow evil and suffering in the world, has been in the hearts of believers for centuries. For unbelievers, theodicy is not their question; rather it is how to live with suffering and evil—a challenge they share with all human beings.[17] Moderns compound this problem by the conviction that they are to bring about universal benevolence through their own efforts. The neighbor no longer lives next door; the neighbor has a global identity. To cope with the demand of "one's neighbor" people act both with responsibility as well as by practising self-protective indifference (LS 25).

Christians and secular humanists struggle with a practical response to evil and suffering more than a theoretical one. Religious share in this struggle. To avoid being overwhelmed, they can refuse to listen to the Evening News. Some may draw a line at who will be included in their concern, to distance themselves from suffering. While there is satisfaction in being able to organize others around a good cause, many, if overwhelmed, will justify limiting the next response. We all recognize ourselves in these coping mechanisms.

More sinister responses also occur. Some adopt an all-powerful solution or group as a response to the evil which they encounter. What is out of reach of this program or ideology is set aside. Even violence can be legitimated in service to this cause. Groups formed in opposition to "evil" may use hostility to the "other" as an element of their own identity. The fingerprint of such identity is its non-dialogical tone.[18] Evil is projected onto others. This "distancing" from evil serves to blur the recognition that all share to some degree in the evil found in the world.

These patterns are in evidence across the globe. New forms of tribalism threaten world peace today. A type of white Christian

---

[17]Taylor, *A Secular Age*, 680–5.
[18]Judith Merkle, *Being Faithful: Christian Commitment in Modern Society* (London: Bloomsbury/T&T Clark, 2010), 147–67.

nationalism attacks democratic institutions.[19] In recent centuries, Christianity and democracy have co-existed through the separation of church and state.[20] Yet today there can be an erasure of the line which separates piety from politics in different sectors of the globe. Instead of fostering Christian values within a country, the language of Christianity is used to gain power, to exclude others, or to wage aggression. This creates an imposter Christianity, which can go undetected unless challenged.[21] "Real citizens" are defined in opposition to those of opposing views; "the people" are those who look like us. Beliefs are stated: this is our nation, our church, our humanity—not theirs, and the desire to take back what is ours is a slogan of aggression.[22] Pope Francis cautions against these tendencies across the world (FT 37–55). These dynamics of the fragmentation of our societies are a response to the problem of evil by locating evil in the "other." Congregations also can experience these patterns of polarization among themselves and their members as they move forward in times of uncertainty and challenge.

Congregational Life

Expressions of fragmentation in religious communities are often more subtle. Religious can fill the need for an underlying ideology of religious life today with attention to a cause, expecting from it a focus and *raison d'etre* it cannot produce. What begins as a sincere desire to address a problem can morph into an all-encompassing purpose. Pope Francis claims that the modern spirit has become sick

---

[19]Philip S. Gorski and Samuel L. Perry, *The Flag and the Cross: White Christian Nationalism and the Threat to American Democracy* (New York: Oxford University Press, 2022).

[20]This separation of church and state has not meant the separation of church and culture, as Catholic Social Teaching directs. See: Judith A. Merkle, *From the Heart of the Church: The Catholic Social Tradition* (Collegevillle, MN: The Liturgical Press, 2004).

[21]See the challenge by the wider Orthodox Church: https://publicorthodoxy.org/2022 /03/13/ a-declaration-on-the-russian-world-russkii-mir teaching/. See also: John Blake, "An Imposter Christianity is Threatening American Democracy," *CNN*, July 24, 2022.

[22]Gorski and Perry, *The Flag and the Cross*, 15.

with the desire for new things (LS 211). Religious might not fill this desire with a new iPhone or wardrobe but might think that one public and eye-catching project will provide for the future of its religious life, attract new members, and regain its relevance. Patricia Wittberg explains that the vacuum left by the dissolution of institutionally-based ministries leads religious to adopt the meanings, ideas, and definitions current in similar groups. Congregations search for other foci from the larger environment, or from their societies at large. "Many of the religious orders and societies thus engaged in mimetic isomorphism, borrowing each other's attempts to articulate new virtuoso spiritualities based on ecological consciousness, Christian or Eastern mysticism, Native America spiritual forms, or even New Age concepts."[23] Organic farms, ecological centers, hermitages, and religious art studies arise at motherhouses—not wrong or bad in themselves, but often with little reasoned connection to each other or to the order's original spiritual focus. These substitute for the absence of an internally coherent group spirituality.[24]

In his exhortation on the modern holiness, Pope Francis claims that the ancient heresies of Gnosticism and Pelagianism remain dangerous in the modern era. Both define a holiness that does not need God. Contemporary forms of Gnosticism reduce Christian holiness to a set of abstract ideas detached from the flesh and the complexity of life. Pope Francis points to the attraction of a "strict and allegedly pure . . . faith [which] can appear to possess a certain harmony or order that encompasses everything" (GE 38). This style or solution can circumvent the complexity of modern evil with a total system, often held as a higher knowledge not available to the common sense of others. The above is coupled with new forms of Pelagianism. Here, salvation and holiness are reduced to our own powers, success, and outward actions, which lead individuals "to feel superior to others because they observe certain rules or remain intransigently faithful to a particular Catholic style" (GE 49). One can be consumed by possession of "higher knowledge," imitating a past triumphal church but with secular coinage. The outcomes of

---

[23]Wittberg, *From Piety to Professionalism and Back?*, 265.
[24]See: Margaret Scott, "Greening the Vows: *Laudato Si* and Religious Life," *The Way* 54, no. 4 (October 2015): 83–93. This is an example of a deeper inquiry into the integral relationship of care for the earth and the life of the vows.

a specific program, a certain liturgical style, or a public issue can become a litmus test of Catholic identity. None of these responses need God or the direction of the Holy Spirit. Without being led by grace, we shift our attention from God and the realization of the Kingdom to ourselves.[25] These are false responses to the problem of evil and suffering.

The illusion of "being right" reinforces a type of exceptionalism and damages community. A lifestyle enclave rather than a community develops to create a preferred "life." In the broader society a lifestyle enclave is based on leisure and consumption and includes only others who share this lifestyle. In religious communities its tenor is more likely spiritual and moral—since "better than" is measured in a different coinage. Religious often refer to these entities as "camps." Robert Bellah illustrates how such enclaves cause fragmentation. "The different, those with other lifestyles, are not necessarily despised. They may be willingly tolerated. But they are irrelevant or even invisible in terms of one's own lifestyle enclave."[26] Lifestyle enclaves are just another weak attempt to insure self-protection in face suffering and evil and the pluralism of the times. The human dilemma is how to separate a response to evil and the doing of good from strategies of exclusion, as well as to meet the needs for understanding and friendship, which we all need.

Living One's Charism

Charism can be a bridge for a congregation into this dialogue. Religious life is a total life in which a *gestalt* of the desire for holiness/spirituality, community/communion with others, and service/works have a relationship to one another. The question of how a congregation responds to evil and witnesses to good shapes its expression of charism in secular times. As an inner self guides the individual in his/her movement toward authenticity, charism shapes

---

[25]Kevin Ahern, "Rejoice and be Glad," *America*, April 30, 2019.
[26]Bellah, *Habits of the Heart*, 70. A lifestyle enclave is focused on private life in which we share only a segment of life, usually leisure and consumption. By contrast, "A community tends to be an inclusive whole, celebrating the interdependence of public and private life and the different callings of all."

the inner self of a congregation. No congregation can do everything, and attention to charism can help them decide how to proceed. The questions regarding the potential impact of charism on its future can only be answered by a congregation itself. Some general lines of inquiry are: what have been characteristic ways of proceeding in congregational history? What values have been priorities? What values guided decisions over time? A second question is how has the congregation functioned as a moral community?[27] What narratives have guided it? In other words, how has it balanced authority and initiative, personal gifts and communal needs, equality and diversity, law and the Spirit, works and community life? What have been mistakes? What have been successes? A third question is what symbols root the group in its identity? When Dorothy Day founded the hospitality houses in the Catholic Worker movement during the Depression, the image of Christ as the homeless person at their door was a compelling symbol for the group. It inspired them to do new things, in challenging times in effective ways. What symbols continue to call the group to investment and service?

Ecclesial Identity before the Question of Good and Evil

Charles Taylor charges there is an eclipse of the agency of God, as one who is active in history, in the modern imagination. The dismissal of God's agency is also a rejection of the Christian concept of communion.[28] The belief in and reality of communion impacts the response to evil and suffering. Communion sums up the meaning of the Christian life as love, as it defines both the nature of God and our relation to God. Moderns reject the idea they have this relationship with God, as well as their need for salvation. Christians hold, on the contrary, that salvation only occurs by our being in communion with God, through the community of humans. Experience of communion is fostered in the church, even though this sense of communion is not supported in secular society.

---

[27]See: Lewis S. Mudge, *The Church as a Moral Community: Ecclesiology and Ethics in Ecumenical Debate* (New York: Continuum, 1998).
[28]Taylor, *A Secular Age*, 279.

Communion identifies Catholic life and the life of a religious congregation. We acknowledge in the Eucharist the creation of a new "we" created in baptism and expressed in the Eucharist: "We pray to you." Yet this "we" is not the self-selected "us" of the lifestyle enclave of modern society. Rather it is the "we" of an identity given to us by Christ, and of the fragile unity capable of being achieved in our relationships with others. In the Eucharist we celebrate that Christ is being raised and continues to raise a body of humanity of which the church is a primary locus only because Christ is first raised by God.[29]

We celebrate that the church then is the servant of humanity to achieve this unity in all the myriad ways its members seek to confront evil and bring about good. We do this with Christ our savior, not just as a moral example, but as a gratuitous gift. In this sense, the Mass is not just useful or real to the extent it mobilizes energies to transform the world. Rather its primary significance is the communication of the gratuitous gift and presence of God in our lives. Congregations, as the whole church, are called by the Eucharist to act ethically through a spiritual offering of both our successes and our failures to accomplish the tasks we seek to accomplish. Because we live as Eucharistic people, we trust that the future of the world does not depend on our efforts alone. We seek from its strength the wisdom to follow a spiritual path of solidarity and communion which develops a new imagination to create systems that are more interdependent in economic, cultural, political, and religious ways. In the Christian life, religious witness that this spiritual path of communion has a political-mystical dimension—it requires trust in God and gives one access to God.

Ordinary Life and Higher Time

The changed sense of time from premodern to modern times creates a second hunger in secular society. In premodern understanding, ordinary or mundane time is transcended by "higher" time—an accounting of time that is not merely linear or chronological.

---

[29]Louis-Marie Chauvet, *The Sacraments: The Word of God at the Mercy of the Body* (Collegeville, MN: The Liturgical Press, 2001), 135–45.

Ancient cultures saw time as cyclical consisting of repeating ages that happen to every being in the Universe from birth to death. Time was also measured differently in the past. In the Middle Ages, daylight was measured in twelve segments; likewise the period of darkness. The hour was loosely defined and was longer in the summer than in the winter. Before the mechanization of time, how time was perceived and regulated could not be separated from local customs, the needs of livestock and crops, and seasons.[30] The world of the Middle Ages was marked also by the unity of church and culture. Feast days punctuated the flow of the year, sacraments marked personal maturation, and work and rest were separated not only by the harvests but by the celebrations which related them to God's providence. Carnival allowed an approved space to let go before a Lenten season of self-discipline and penance.

Secular time, in an immanent frame, has changed this. "We have constructed an environment in which we live in a uniform univocal secular time, which we try to measure and control in order to get things done."[31] The great advantage of universally mechanized time is that millions of people—including those at great distances from one another—can be coordinated in their actions, simply by telling each of them what time to act. We try still, through routines and narratives, to distinguish one time from another: public commemorations, annual events, sports seasons, long weekends, travel, and hobbies. However, these substitutes are fragile before the rituals and narratives of premodern "higher" times, which not only measured changes in time but gave them meaning.

The world of entertainment and travel has grown in proportion to the fear of boredom in the culture. People plan long weekends to break the cycle of going to work, sleeping, and going to work again. A woman applying to a volunteer organization commented she belonged to seven bridge clubs at once and wanted something meaningful to do with her time. The international pandemic forced many into a suspension of time through isolation. The "great resignation" in some first-world societies reflects the questions people posed to the work-to-life ratio they had adopted. The

---

[30]Mary Froelich, *Breathed into Wholeness: Catholicity and Life in the Spirit* (New York, Orbis Books, 2019), 56–8.
[31]Taylor, *A Secular Age*, 59.

pandemic fostered a reappraisal of how moderns use time and stimulated the desire to re-examine the meaning of time into some new kind of whole.[32]

The meaning of time becomes most acute when facing death. The pandemic brought unexpected death into many families and communities. A closed world offers little meaning for the passing of time marked by death, beyond the hope one will be remembered in the future. Yet, the "longing" for a sense of eternity arises spontaneously at moments of a family death or similar experiences. Taylor comments that this "doesn't show that the faith perspective is correct. It just shows that the yearning for eternity is not the trivial and childish thing it is painted as."[33] An immanent frame simply offers the markers of a life course to give sense to life's meaning. For some, though, it gives rise to the question, is this all there is?

Pope Francis ties the mindset of the "technocratic paradigm" to the avoidance of asking the meaning of our time on earth. Disregard for the earth, indifference to the poor, and seeing everything from a utilitarian perspective provide an encompassing mindset which fosters the use of people and creation in the service of self-interest.[34] A false view of the human condition is reinforced by the assumption that human problems can be solved solely through the right technology. The technocratic paradigm clouds the meaning of death, the recognition of the truths and limits of creation, and the wider purpose of goods in the economy. In their place it offers belief in the quick fix. It fosters the assumption that technology will provide the answer to our unlimited expectations. Humans need no eternity to complete what is missing. The technocratic paradigm denies the limit to life that all humans share and cannot defeat. Death is made just another choice—one that needs no other framework of meaning. As Pope Francis puts it, "When human beings place themselves at the center, they give absolute priority to immediate convenience and all else becomes relative"—everything is "irrelevant unless it services one's own immediate interests" (LS 122). There are

---

[32]Ibid., 720.

[33]Ibid.

[34]Anthony Annett, "The Economic Vision of Pope Francis," in *The Theological and Ecological Vision of Laudato Si'*, ed. Vincent Miller (London: Bloomsbury/T&T Clark, 2017), 165.

moments in life however when this framework wears thin. It is at these times, Taylor asserts, that moderns ask what it is all about.

The sacramental order of the church attempts to bridge the gap between God, ourselves, and the world. It is one way higher time and ordinary time are linked. The sacramental order is a symbolic order: it requires the subjection of one partner to the other. The symbol can provide an order in which I find my meaning by finding my place within it, a meaning bigger than myself.[35] A sacramental outlook presents the Christian life in relationship to the life, death, and resurrection of Jesus Christ. The paschal mystery, sharing in the death and resurrection of Jesus Christ, is its primary lens. The narrative of the path of Jesus becomes a paradigm for the narrative of one's own life.

The church recognizes the idea of "sacramentality" more broadly than identification of the seven sacraments. The church itself is "sacrament." The church speaks of the "sacramentality of creation."[36] The action of Christians for justice in the world has a "sacramental" dimension. John Paul II remarked that as we find worth in our neighbor, respond to her or him as "other" we find God. The bonds formed in this way are deeper than the natural or human bonds we hope bind the world (SRS 40). Christian faith is not only one of personal immediacy with God, it functions through the signs and symbols of the church. The liturgical seasons of the church serve to link ordinary time with higher time.

Religious Congregations

Religious congregations certainly have a "sacramental" presence and meaning in the church and the world. Religious vows are not one of the seven sacraments. The elements which make up religious life, as an adult lifestyle in the church, have a sacramental significance, though. They can provide a witness to the meaning of time over

---

[35]Chauvet, *The Sacraments*, 147.
[36]Kevin Irwin, "The Sacramentality of Creation and the Role of Creation in the Liturgy and Sacraments," in *And God Saw That It Was Good: Catholic Theology and the Environment*, ed. Drew Christenson and Walter E. Grazer (Washington, DC: United States Catholic Conference, 1996).

a life course. The value of a celibate life stance is hard to answer if this life is all there is. Life in an immanent frame cannot support putting aside the establishment of a personal economic future, living in a shared economy, simple lifestyle, and commitment to fostering economic justice. The vow of obedience can seem to challenge the importance that decisions which affect one's life are only chosen directly. Yet personal decisions have little meaning unless some options are more significant than others. Without some measure beyond choice itself, the very idea of self-choice falls into triviality and hence incoherence.[37] Religious enter communal decision-making because they have a purpose to accomplish, a common good, which can only be accomplished with others. Practices of religious life are concrete interpretations of the gospel, which flow from its lifestyle. The structure of the life makes concrete one way to pay attention to transcendence in decision-making, in solidarity, and service with and for others. Acceptance of the constraints and possibilities of community life requires believing that living within boundaries and limits will enhance, not ruin, your life. Religious vows witness that the ideal of self-choice supposes that there are other issues of significance beyond self-choice. Independent of my will there is something noble, worth my effort, and hence offers significance in giving shape to my own life. One way to name this is the Kingdom of God; love for neighbor and union with God. The sacramentality of religious life, as public witness, gives flesh to these beliefs and grounds its identity in the wider sacramentality of the church.

The seven sacraments are not magical, moral rewards or a way to control God, or the otherness of God which ultimately gives meaning to life.[38] John Paul II cautions against both an over-evaluation of the sacraments as the sole maker of a "practicing Christian" and an over-evaluation of ethics—political or emotional or charismatic—as our "wedding garment" of salvation. The love and mercy of God, shown forth in the Eucharist, offer what is more powerful than evil and death: the ultimate contingency before time.

---

[37]Taylor, *The Ethics of Authenticity*, 39.
[38]Louis-Marie Chauvet, *Symbols and Sacrament: A Sacramental Reinterpretation of Christian Existence*, trans. Patrick Madigan, S.J. and Madeleine Beaumont (Collegeville, MN: The Liturgical Press, 1992), 173–7.

It counters the apparent limitations of the ordinariness and limits of life with the offer of God's own love. This sacramental celebration conveys an ongoing meaning that qualifies all meanings we attempt to put on life. Even our notion of what justice is has to receive a new content through being exposed to the only creative power of love which is more powerful than sin: God's love (DM 14). This is the ongoing process of Christian existence, of which the sacraments are one part.

In secular society, the sacraments are not automatic experiences of God. A challenge to theology today is how to convey their value in terms which are understood in a new society.[39] The spiritual senses required to encounter God in the sacraments involve not just thinking spiritual thoughts but making room for God, giving God freedom of action—surrender. Love of neighbor is the practice which impacts our awareness of sacramental presence and the meaning it conveys for our lives.[40] The effort of creative action in charity and the collaboration necessary for the common good give meaning. In both love of neighbor and worship, men and women move to second place, and God stands before them in the first place. The sacraments speak of the eschatological *in between time*. It is the time of an "already"—God is present in life with the gift of salvific love—and a *not yet*; all human meaning we place in this world is not complete. They are *witnesses of a God who is never finished with coming:* a God who submits to be present through the passage of concrete signs and symbols in time of which the sacraments are a trace.[41]

Charism

How might the charism of a congregation help it to respond to this life question of modern life—the relationship of ordinary time to higher

---

[39]See for example: "Sacramental Presence in a Postmodern Context-Fundamental Theological Approaches" LEST-Leuven Encounters in Systematic Theology. http://www.lestconference.com/

[40]Mark McInroy, *Balthasar on the Spiritual Senses: Perceiving Splendour* (Oxford and New York: Oxford University Press, 2014).

[41]Chauvet, *Symbol and Sacrament,* 565.

time? Within the congregation, questions of time are meaningful to its life, mission, and future; among them are: What time is it for us? Are we just beginning? It is time to pass on our charism to another generation. What do we need to do this? Who will do this? A second is, what do we need to have a public presence that others can observe today? Do we need to engage in collaborative efforts to meet current needs? Is our mission completed? A third question is, what rituals do we need to help members understand their identity and mission now? While all religious congregations share in the sacramental life of the church, the prayer traditions which are internal to the group are important. Rituals are needed in communities that are inclusive of cultural identities, connect members to its spiritual traditions, respect the need for both masculine and feminine expressions of belonging, and link social concerns to the spiritual life of the group. Religious communities can be places where others can ritualize how their life course and situation relate to faith. Religious can foster faith development among persons through sponsorship of centers of spirituality and events. Historically, the practice of devotions in the church addressed the need for forms of prayer to connect daily needs to a life of faith.[42] Renewed forms of spirituality can foster the strong emotional appeals which have helped people through the years to function in changed circumstances in real time. Religious congregations can contribute to this renewal in spirituality which helps to relate ordinary and higher times.

Points of Contact with Fullness

A third spiritual hunger of secular times is the need to articulate fullness. Fullness is a sense of the transcendent or encounter with mystery. The challenge today is to connect the experience of being drawn to fullness to the unity of the experience to which it points. Moderns often experience "conversion," or change in their lives, as simply a natural occurrence. It is common that as people grow emotionally, intellectually, and in other areas, they explain these changes as accounted for in their own terms, without a sense of

---

[42]Robert Orsi, *Thank You Saint Jude: Women's Devotion to the Patron Saint of Hopeless Causes* (New Haven, CT: Yale University Press, 1998).

transcendence.[43] In modern mentality, there is no need to go beyond the natural to understand the world and all human experience. The desire to meet the supernatural in the natural is set aside or met with silence.

One author describes the experience of fullness or transcendence in ordinary experience as if you are standing in a room where you hear music, but do not know its source.[44] A person can feel uneasy in this experience because to identify the source as transcendent bucks the system of generally accepted language. Acknowledgment of more than a coincidence present can discredit one's modernity, suggest a regression to a premodern understanding of life or a childish outlook. So, people remain silent. For active believers, a similar experience can confirm personal belief. Still others, even if they have discarded a previous religious background, may believe again. In secular times it is not uncommon for people to sort through their exposure to several belief systems acquired throughout their lives, and dig deeper for the possibility or renewed contact with a transcendent partner. Pope Francis refers to this experience as an encounter in modern faith. The opposite of such an encounter is dismissal: to immerse oneself in the affairs of the ordinary, and not attend to any greater significance at all.

Both believers and unbelievers search for contact with fullness, or "the more." Being a believer does not mean a person is always conscious of their connection to their Source. There are a wide range of moments in life, and stances, between belief and unbelief. Pope Francis offers an image of the church as a polyhedron, one that must embrace a great diversity of stages and moments of belief and unbelief. A polyhedron is not a sphere, rather a solid having many sides. A polyhedron lacks the harmony of the sphere but retains the unity of a solid. It offers variable distances from its center and not a single way of being related to it.[45] While the identity of the church always requires defined boundaries established by its tradition and

---

[43]Taylor, *The Secular Age*, 732.
[44]Bernard Lonergan, S.J., *Method in Theology* (Toronto: University of Toronto Press, 1990), 290, with reference of Oliver Rabut, *Experience religieuse fundamentale* (Tournai: Castermann, 1968), 168.
[45]Matt Kappadakunnel, "Reframing the Catholic Spectrum into a Polyhedron," *Catholic Outlook*, December 19, 2020. See also: *Evangelii Gaudium* (236), *Querida Amazonia* (28), *Fratelli Tutti* (146, 190, 215).

internal law, Pope Francis recognizes that we do not share the same unity of culture that engaged the church at Vatican II. Secular times require the church to encounter a great variety of postures in the search for faith today.

Within religious congregations, this same diversity exists. There is a hunger to integrate the diverse experiences modern religious life has offered members into the core faith expression and language of congregational life. When new members approach congregations, their own diversity on this sacred/secular continuum brings issues of race, class, gender, and ethnicity to specify what "doors" will foster contact with fullness for them. Attention to these new conditions of faith helps all members to experience a deeper and transformative encounter with God and to share it with others.

Taylor remarks that those without a religious background but open to the transcendent can find God in new ways through others. Some, in the absence of a direct experience, "may take on a view about religion from others: saints, prophets, charismatic leaders, who have radiated some sense of more direct contact."[46] They can sense that others have been closer or more familiar with what they seek. The confidence necessary to take a new step in articulating fullness can be drawn from a shared religious language. Religious communities can foster exposure to these experiences. The interpretation of these stirrings relies on a faith community, as the immanent stance of the culture offers no language for them. Whether "conversion" arises in the experience of a believer, or one who never believed, it will involve a change of heart. There is a transformation of the frame in which people thought or lived before. "They bring into view something beyond that frame, which at the same time changes the meaning of all the elements of the frame. Things make sense in a new way."[47] When Taylor looks into the future he foresees two directions secular conversion experience may take. Both have implications for the future of religious congregations.

In the first case, there will be a shift in societies where the general atmosphere leans toward an immanent frame for explaining life's purpose. Even though many people have trouble understanding how a sane person could believe in God, the dominant secularization

---

[46]Taylor, *A Secular Age*, 729.
[47]Ibid., 731.

narrative, which blames our religious past for many of the woes of our world, will become less plausible over time. They will notice that other societies are not following suit and will also experience internal pressures of the adequacy of this explanation. At the same time, the atmosphere of immanence, and sense that this is all there is, will intensify a sense of living in a "wasteland" for subsequent generations.[48] Many young people will begin to explore beyond the limitations of the immanent frame. The emptiness of the present, coupled with the persistent pressure of a sense of transcendence that cannot be explained away, will continue to generate a search for "the more" in its deepest sense, beyond the paucity of "this is all there is."

A "spiritual" but not religious path might be a stage in this quest but ultimately will not contain it. Here the role of the church comes to light in a new way. The purpose of the church is to witness to the Kingdom, the mystery "not visible" to the naked eye yet expressed within the concrete nature of everyday experience. Mystery itself within the ordinary shifts our everyday meanings—the fulcrum of the paradigm changes. The church, its membership, and religious life itself can be a point of contact with fullness, a response to the third spiritual hunger.

Church as Mediation

The principle of mediation is a distinguishing characteristic of the church and one at the core of its identity. Mediation means what is most spiritual always takes place in what is most corporeal. Chauvet claims that one becomes Christian only by entering an institution. Faith is lived in a tradition, a history of relationships, in an institution in a religious form. As institutional, it is doctrinal, moral, ritual, and so on. Faith is not only a personal reality which I construct. Rather faith and the experience which gives rise to it require an interpretation.[49] The modes of Christian behavior which appear the most "personal" such as meditative prayer, or

---

[48]Ibid., 770.
[49]Hans Joas, *Do We Need Religion?* trans. Alex Skinner (London: Paradigm, 2008), 46, 53.

the most "authentic" such as concern for others, are always the
expression of an apprenticeship interiorized for a long time and of
habits inculcated by institutional and highly ritualized processes.[50]
People understand themselves as Christians, speak of themselves
as Christians, and lead Christian lives only because of the church,
and through the mediation of the body, within the body of a society
or context of life. Religious life also is rooted in this mediation.
The church too exists in a posture of mediation. The fundamental
dependence of the church on its Lord is expressed in the Eucharist.[51]

How the church, as well as religious congregations, fosters
religious identity is key to its effectiveness as a mediator before
the hungers of secular society, especially that of contact with
fullness. Secular society does not link people to the sacred in any
broader framework, whether through the "church" or the state. For
moderns, personal identity itself is free-floating. Identity no longer
flows from the experience of common action with others, as "I
belong to this group." It often arises simply from a simultaneous
mutual presence of mutual display.[52] Mutual display is not the same
as belonging. Modern consumer society is full of spaces of "display"
rather than belonging. The giant malls of today are meta-topical
places which link us through commodities to an imagined higher
existence elsewhere. I wear Nike shoes, and through that display I
am a person who just does it!

Youth today attach to consumer identity, movie stars, the right
music, a huge role in their sense of self, which displaces in many
cases the importance of belonging to large-scale collective agencies
like nations and churches, political parties, or groups for advocacy.
These collectives or communities are different from occasions of
mutual display. They have the capacity to uphold commonly
enforced virtues of character. Values of hard work and productivity,
family values, and service are linked to these frameworks of
belonging. Mutual display only carries superficial and temporary
bonds.

What does this mean for the church? Obviously in all its
forms, the Christian church has traditionally been an advocate of

[50]Chauvet, *The Sacraments*, 25.
[51]Merkle, *Being Faithful: Christian Commitment in Modern Society*, 88–90.
[52]Taylor, *A Secular Age*, 481; see also: 481–7.

mechanisms of belonging and identity beyond the superficiality of "mutual display." It can offer, as an alternative, "itineraries" of Christian lives of fullness and attention to conscience. Both have the potential to ground people in moral sources which can support a life beyond the goals of a "closed system" and an order of mutual benefit. International capitalism produces "a culture of indifference" which proves problematic for modern identity if it is not counterbalanced by a practice which challenges it.[53] The church therefore must offer a clear picture of the meaning of life, as one religious put it, something which does not expire. Taylor argues that "the unity of the church as stretching into eternity across all ages of time" offers "paradigm itineraries" gathered from its living traditions, which "cannot be identified with those of any one age."[54]

Finally, attention to the importance of the human conscience is necessary for the church to be an effective mediator before the hungers of secular society. A robust sense of conscience in religious congregations therefore is a necessity.[55] One does not have to choose between personal conscience and membership in the church. The actual credibility of the church is linked to the recognition of the freedom of conscience in a secular age. Pope Francis refers to the teaching of Vatican II when he describes conscience as, "the interior place for listening to the truth, to goodness, for listening to God. It is the inner place of my relationship to God, the One who speaks to my heart and helps me to discern, to understand the way I must take and, once the decision is made, to go forward, to stay faithful."[56] Conscience is a primary avenue for contact with fullness, the mystery which grounds the unity of experience, ultimately God. While the church is a voice for human dignity in secular life, some of its positions conflict with popular sentiment, and an impasse

---

[53]Vincent Miller, *Consuming Religion: Christian Faith and Practice in Consumer Culture* (New York: Continuum, 2004).

[54]Taylor, *A Secular Age*, 830, note 64. Hans Joas, *Faith as an Option,* trans. Alex Skinner (Stanford, CA: Stanford University Press, 2014) offers possible futures for Christianity in Europe, see: 126–43.

[55]See the essays in *Conscience and Catholic Health Care: From Clinical Contexts to Governmental Mandates,* ed. David E. DeCosse and Thomas A. Nairn, O.F.M (Maryknoll, NY: Orbis Books, 2017).

[56]"Conscience Means Listening to God," *Angelus Address,* St. Peter's Square, June 30, 2013.

develops between church and society.[57] On one hand, the secular situation opens space for the church to step in and be a voice for an ethical path for contemporary society. On the other hand, the church must search to formulate its moral teachings attentive to the truth of the gospel, the tradition, human experience as well as available knowledge. In this, the church cannot ignore the real struggles toward human fulfillment experienced in modern life, nor characterize the views that dominate public life in general as misguided without recognizing they often represent conflicting truth claims (AL 38).

It is important for religious congregations to respect the consciences of its own members as well as others. This is necessary for the collaboration required for its mission. While concern over subjectivism not guided by a more objective morality is real (LS 217), there also needs to be a concern for the conscience of persons for ministry and witness to be effective. Evolving experience in the human community can challenge other sources of moral knowledge, and the church has a key role in deciphering the modern, psychoanalytic, and political categories which lurk under the veneer of both secular and ecclesiastical debates.[58] The church, as well as religious congregations, will be an effective mediator before the hungers of secular society as it fosters the capacity of judgment which rings true to the human capacity to recognize the truth of things, be drawn to the good, and identify the Spirit alive in the world.

Charism and Contact with Fullness

The founding charism of every religious congregation can be a beacon to those who search for fullness in society today. Its attraction to members for generations rests in its capacity to bear witness

---

[57]Jose Casanova, "The Contemporary Disjunctions between Social and Church Morality," in *Church and Peoples: Disjunctions in a Secular Age*, ed. Charles Taylor, Jose Casanova and George F. McLean (Washington, DC: The Council for Research in Values and Philosophy, 2012), 127–35.
[58]Sara Coakley, *The New Asceticism: Sexuality, Gender and the Quest for God* (London: Bloomsbury, 2013), 140.

to something real in the God–human relationship. No single work of a congregation; education, health care, social work, pastoral work; nor one cause, ecological commitment, racial equality, equal rights, hunger, peacekeeping, etc., is sufficient to ground a full congregational identity. The "deep story" of a congregation also speaks to the unmet spiritual hungers of secular times along with its concrete expression in ministry. Both witness God's presence of healing and grace in the secular world. As congregations sense the Spirit at this moment in history, they stand in moments of knowing and not knowing the way ahead. Yet they also can expect the reassurance promised to the Body of Christ. As in Paul's prayer in Ephesians, we are promised in every age the "fullness of the one who fills all things in every way" (Eph. 1:23). In new times congregations know, "There is in the world, as it were a charged field of love and meaning, here and there it reaches a notable intensity; but it is ever unobtrusive, hidden, inviting each of us to join. And join we must if we are to perceive it, for our perceiving is through our own loving."[59]

---

[59]Bernard J. Lonergan, S.J., *Method in Theology* (Toronto: University of Toronto Press, 1990), with reference to Rabut, *Experience religieuse fondamentale*, 168.

6

Adaptations for a New Environment

Adaptation in nature indicates the ways life grows and develops before the possibility of death and extinction. Ice plants in the desert overcame an environment with scarce water resources by establishing new patterns from within to absorb water. Their adaptive behavior did not require an ideal situation; it was shaped by its semi-arid environment. Specific adaptations ensured survival and the reproduction necessary to create a new species. It would be wonderful to move from this analogical lens upon nature to make specific predictions and remedies for religious congregations and their future directions. Yet there is no single solution for its development. In nature, transitions often depend on a key element needed for survival. In religious life there are various positions on the "one thing necessary" for its future.

The list of ideas is extensive: more new members, increased funds for projects, and a clear apostolate. Others claim a need for a more hospitable church, better family life, or a renewal of community living. A third group focuses on "right thinking" of various types: an intercultural-interracial mindset, a new cosmology, theological renewal, environmental consciousness, democratic decision-making, the use of social analysis, and so on. There is no consensus among religious regarding "the one thing necessary" for adaptation to a secular society. In practice, many congregations struggle with the concerns of the here and now. Despite diversity of outlook, religious believe their lives witness the universal presence of divine healing and grace which embraces our world. Hope animates congregations to "sense the Spirit" and search for the path where the Spirit may lead them. Their love grounds the energy to meet the challenges involved in this journey with generous hearts.

Religious share a challenge with many across the world: the need to survive, to face the unprecedented demand to be creative in a new world. In *Fratelli Tutti*, Pope Francis warns that anyone who thinks that the only lesson to be learned in modern times is the need to improve what we are already doing or to refine existing systems and regulations is denying reality (FT 7). Men and women across the world struggle with the crosswinds of doubt, uncertainty, and fear as they face the future. Unfamiliar pressures within nations, unstable world systems, a shifting balance of power, need for alternative forms of energy and unprecedented situations of disease and healing contest established approaches. Religious experience these same tensions. When doubt, uncertainty, and fear take over the lives of congregations, they are threats to the faith, hope, and love which is the glue of religious life. While religious lack answers to our future, they know the gifts available to search for it. Without renewed faith, hope, and love it is possible that congregations will be crippled by the same forces which paralyze the social and geopolitical world. Attainable goals and available capacities to move forward are blocked by the fear of change and the inability to act in solidarity. To enter communal discernment regarding their future, religious need the freedom necessary to do so.

The importance of the communal dimension of religious life has new significance as religious share challenges with people across the world. A community is not just a number of people within a geographical frontier. It is an achievement of common meaning at different levels of life realized by decisions and choices, especially over the long term. As religious devise ways to meet the challenges before them, to avoid the easy exits on the journey, they must act in solidarity, even though this is difficult. Their movement together is an icon of the healing and creating in history that signifies God's presence in the world. The gifts of faith, hope, and love—the theological virtues—function to animate the needed decisions. This chapter will look more deeply into how they make a difference.

Faith before Doubt: Living Ordinary Life with an Eye on Higher Time

Classically doubt is the state in which the mind is suspended between two contradictory ideas—unable to assent to either of them. Secular society is no stranger to doubt and uncertainty. People seek a sense of transcendence while at the same time asking how the experience of being drawn to fullness is linked to a greater reality. The world in which they live, however, holds "this is all there is."[1] Author Flannery O'Connor names this uncertainty as: "the conflict between an attraction for the Holy and the disbelief in it that we breathe in the air of our times."[2] Often doubt is associated with intellectual problems of faith, morals, or truth claims. However, doubt has another unacknowledged expression: today it touches the existential level of life. Students ask in the classroom, is this true? How do you know? Some news channels and politicians announce a "post truth" society, conveying that this is acceptable. A climate of doubt feeds the abandonment of the search for purpose in life. It fosters the attitude that meaning is fluid and depends on opinion alone.

Doubt and Bias

Theologian Bernard Lonergan views the cycle of human life through a lens of progress, decline, and redemption. Doubt cripples the trust and clarity needed for relationships with others. Doubt and bias lie at the heart of community breakdown. Bias interferes with the open-mindedness essential for any communal progress. Bias and doubt do not just slow down progress, they cause paralysis. Doubt, caused by partial knowledge, is not the danger. Questioning leads to greater knowledge and informed action, steps toward the truth. Doubt is insidious when it blocks truth-seeking and the search is avoided. Decline results.

---

[1]Charles Taylor, *A Secular Age* (Cambridge, MA: The Belknap Press of Harvard University, 2007), 732.
[2]As quoted by Richard Gilman, "A Life of Letters," *The New York Times*, March 18, 1979.

As a theologian, Lonergan recognizes that the decline caused by doubt is a manifestation of bias and part of the power of sin. Many forms of alienation flow from bias. In bias, self-transcendence is not only bypassed, "reasons" which uphold its refusal are given. Since progress relies on attentive, intelligent, reasonable, and responsible cooperation, decline flows from the refusal to cooperate and the biased reasons given to defend it. The desire to know, to raise relevant questions, and to try to understand something as completely as possible is repressed to avoid the self-giving of cooperation. This is the work of bias which stagnates individuals and communities.

Unlike ice plants in the desert, human beings do not adapt to new situations simply through instinctual impulses, they also must freely choose to do so. This requires recognizing bias and confronting it. Egoism limits an individual's questioning to only those things which contribute to one's own point of view. The merit of every new situation is evaluated by its suitability to his or her need alone. Groups can have a corporate bias, a type of group egotism and blindness, expressed as generational, racial, cultural, or tribal. A situation is ignored or a remedy dismissed to the degree it limits the group power or, in some cases, the power group. Bias is reflected in the insistence on immediate results, which detracts from working toward values and goals which are long in coming.[3] The antidote to bias is the search for authenticity by individuals and groups. It is the consistent struggle to be attentive, intelligent, reasonable, and responsible in face of inattentiveness, obtuseness, unreasonableness, and irresponsibility.[4] Addressing bias on the one hand is an act of the will; on the other hand, it is evidence of grace. It is a practice of openness to the Holy Spirit, who is beyond our capacity to experience. Active and intentional participation in collaboration with the Spirit often comes as a surprise. Yet it is a moment of grace which we can refuse or ignore. For this reason, we often recount these experiences of the Spirit's transforming

---

[3]See: Judith A. Merkle, *Beyond Our Lights and Shadows: Charism and Institution in the Church* (London: Bloomsbury/T&T Clark, 2016), 10–14.
[4]Bernard Lonergan, S.J., "Healing and Creating in History," in *The Lonergan Reader*, ed. Mark D. Morelli and Elizabeth A. Morelli (Murray) (Toronto: University of Toronto Press, 1997), 136–8.

presence as being "moved"—being led to where we might not go on our own. A fruit of such experience is that we are led to seek out others and practices which will support movement toward the vision we glimpsed in that experience.[5]

While authenticity involves intellectual, affective, and moral changes on a day-by-day basis, "qualitative leaps" of significant change therefore can occur. Lonergan disagrees with modern thinkers who maintain that repression, alienation, or domination in groups are such total states they cannot be transformed.[6] To the contrary, longtime patterns of thinking and behavior which condition even our assessment of our human condition can change. There can be a "breakthrough;" the new can occur. Today religious life is at a juncture—it can move forward or decline. Some feel the changes made after Vatican II are sufficient for the future, another change is not necessary or even possible. Yet others recognize that congregations face a different time than the post-Vatican II church. They want their congregations to discern what needs to be done and exhibit a new realism.

A New Realism in Secular Times

A new realism emerges as a truth which exists beyond a situation of doubt and apparent contradiction. The realism reflects a larger order which encompasses both parts of the apparent contradiction. The emptiness of the present, coupled with a sense of transcendence that cannot be explained away, continues to generate new options in society.[7] Religious share in this movement of the Spirit as they seek to create new avenues to the future. They can read statistics of decline as well as believe in the coming of the Kingdom. Neither those who say "yes" to the future or refuse to do so can prove their point beyond all doubt.

Flannery O'Connor acknowledged this ambiguity in her writing. She believed in "the point not visible" to the naked eye but believed in firmly. She sought to expose in her writing a type of realism which

---

[5]Mary Frohlich, *Breathed into Wholeness: Catholicity and Life in the Spirit* (New York: Orbis Books, 2019), 149.
[6]Merkle, *Beyond Our Lights and Shadows*, 73.
[7]Judith A. Merkle, *Discipleship, Secularity and the Modern Self: Dancing to Silent Music* (London: Bloomsbury/T&T Clark, 2020), 217.

some found "grotesque." The "point not visible" for O'Connor was the truth of religion amid its unhealthy patterns in the 1950s in the United States. O'Connor challenged the conventional thinking that those who stood outside formal practices of religion and "polite society" were damned. She depicted the outcasts and despised in culture as often closer to God. The realism sought by religious today is an expression of this same "point not visible" in their lives. It may only have tentative answers yet its pursuit engages the public witness of religious life as a sign. Certainty of life's ultimate future grounds the efforts of religious to be witnesses to God's healing and creating history in this time of transition. The move forward requires a renewed simplicity of heart and prayer for a deeper authenticity for the journey.

A New Context: An Age of Contingency

What worked for people in the past to articulate life's depths and meaning, "can today feel remote, tired, and incapable of nourishing the spirit."[8] People find it hard to pinpoint why this is so or explain just how our times are different from those of the past. One approach to indicate the difference between today and the past is the reference to current times as "an age of contingency."

We call contingent that which is neither necessary nor impossible. A theory of contingency characterizes the present age by underlining the increased options for individual action. Behaviors which were necessary through custom or lack of options in the past are optional today, with no "counterforce" or necessity to require them.[9] Contingency in religious life can be experienced in the absence of institutional ministries which once mapped in almost an absolute form what was expected of a religious. Religious life itself does not require any one set of circumstances for its existence. It has existed in various systems and shares with the persistence of religion an endurance in a variety of conditions, despite predictions of its demise.[10]

---

[8]Merkle, *Discipleship, Secularity and the Modern Self*, 70.
[9]Han Joas, *Do We Need Religion?* trans. Alex Skinner (London: Paradigm, 2008), 30.
[10]Hans Joas, *Faith as an Option: Possible Futures for Christianity*, trans. Alex Skinner (Stanford, CA: Stanford University Press, 2014), 71. See also: Jose Casanova,

Karl Rahner refers to a climate of contingency in church and society when he remarks society today no longer sets up concrete guidelines for all its groups. Secular society in the past, while not identical to the Christian life, was more in harmony with it. Society itself was homogenous, hierarchically structured, and with common enough public opinions to shape people's individual decisions about their lives. The impact of society on individuals was less ambiguous than today. In this broader socially-constructed society, Christianity possessed a certain official status. The Christian character of society was a product of and an element in the unity and homogeneousness of a type of secular society which encompassed it. Even though people had to make a personal act of faith within this culture, the culture itself was formed by more amicable factors outside Christianity.[11] A climate of contingency is the experience of the absence of this context. What was necessary or expected in the past might not even be raised today. For instance if, in a church-going family in this former context, a late adolescent stopped going to church, he or she would usually have to explain themselves to their family. Today, the question may not be raised.

Religious life since Vatican II made deep structural changes to adapt to this new world. It sought to modernize and "fix" outdated patterns which no longer served the flourishing of its members or its capacity to serve the world. Yet it is possible that religious congregations also retained an unconscious identification with a world system in which most of its members came of age. The claim that the religious realm was superior to the secular realm was generally accepted in this world. Secularity is the historical process whereby the dualism between these worlds breaks down. The separation between this world and the next remains a matter of faith. However, in the dominant imagination there is only one world: "this world." Religion, as well as religious life, must find its place in the secular world, not the other way around. In this secular world the whole Christian community seeks to express what it

Public Religions in the Modern World (Chicago, IL: The University of Chicago Press, 1994). Here he offers five case studies which demonstrate examples of constrasting situations of religion internationally.
[11]Karl Rahner, "The Situation of Faith Today," in *The Practice of Faith: A Handbook of Contemporary Spirituality* (New York: Crossroad, 1983), 29–32.

knows to be true about life and its meaning. This is the only world in which religious life can express its faith. Jose Casanova puts it this way: "If before, it was the religious realm which appeared to be the all-encompassing reality within which the secular realm found its proper place, now the secular sphere will be the all-encompassing reality, to which the religious sphere will have to adapt."[12] Faith in this world is an option, not a necessity.[13]

Living in Two Worlds

This is a time of transition. We live neither in the past world nor in the future world. The past society still has remnants which need to be maintained and transformed in this new situation to authentically represent the values still needed by the People of God. On the other hand, the core spirit and witness of these forms must be re-expressed in accord with this new age. To just cling to the old is not renewal, nor is making religious life synonymous with standards of society enough. Doubt sneaks into this situation through the covert assumption that religious life itself is part of the old which must pass away. Doubt is sown also when the place of religious life and the rationale for its existence is held up to the yardstick of its past glory, tossing aside the need to re-express its deeper meaning in new forms. When we operate by this standard, questions of doubt are not only formed but also give rise to the wrong questions or assumptions. These questions include whether religious are no longer needed since the state has taken up the ministry of health care and education. Religious life has no value since young people today have other outlets for careers and projects which serve others and advocate for the betterment of society. Doubt raises the question: why make vows? It spawns the assumption that, since communities have other forms of membership such as associates, these are sufficient to allow people to find a sense of belonging without full membership. Even the universal call to holiness of Vatican II generates questions. If the grace sufficient for sanctity is made available to all the Christian faithful in each and every state

---

[12]Ibid., 15.
[13]Joas, *Faith as an Option*, op. cit.

of life (LG 40), why be religious? The answer of necessity, religious life as a "state of perfection," does not distinguish religious life from other states of life, as it once did. Neither is it convincing on an existential level in an age of contingency.[14]

Beyond the State of Perfection

Ernest Larkin observed after the Council that religious life was defined in different terms: "The state of perfection is bypassed and the emphasis shifted from the juridic to the vital reality of grace and charity."[15] This definition goes beyond the institutional questions which once were asked regarding religious congregations. Are you a teaching congregation or a nursing one? Does your congregation have brothers and priests? Are you diocesan or international? Are you missionaries or work in the home country?

A starting point for identifying a vocation to religious life in an age of contingency is the certainty that the faith required of the Christian of the future will be the same faith which can sustain a religious life (LG 30). It is unlikely that the faith of a religious will be different from a faithful member of the parish, or those who are married, or that the faith of the priest will be different from the laity. The circumstances of expressing faith will be different, as well as the obligations of one's state in life, but the faith will be the same.[16] The faith of everyone—priests, religious, married, and single people—in the church will not, in the future, be one developed from a church sustained by a homogenously Christian society. This society which has sustained faith previously is only one possible context of faith, but it is not the only one. The faith which will sustain the life of the church of the future will be one made up of those who have struggled against their environment to reach a personally clear and explicitly responsible decision of faith. Baptism, the core of all vocations in the church, will be lived out in this context, not a

[14]For how this is outlined in the Summa, see: Gregory Pine, O.P. "Religious Life as a State of Perfection," *Nova et Vetera*, English Edition 19, no. 4 (2021): 1181–214.
[15]Ernest Larkin, "Religious Life and Vatican II," *The Sword*, 26 (February 1966): 30–6, at 30.
[16]Karl Rahner, "Fraternal Faith," in *The Practice of Faith: A Handbook of Contemporary Spirituality* (New York: Crossroad, 1983), 32–7.

previous one. People will not be seeking a state of perfection; rather a lifestyle which facilitates and confirms the meaning of the posture which they have taken toward the whole of life and their place in it. The Christian life itself is the pure and healthy development of the stance of a baptized person in relationship to Jesus Christ. The faith which embraces it will be based on the conviction that a fulfilled life is one beyond the flourishing in this life, yet also affirms that full human flourishing involves union with God, as well as full engagement in this world. This faith will be a "yes" to the meaning of life itself as confirmed by the gospel. It will hold the conviction that a life dedicated to others in this life in love is the only truly fulfilling life.[17] Religious life is a life choice based on grace and charity.[18]

Faith to Walk in the Secular World

The life of religious involves a plurality of worlds: congregational, ecclesial, professional, cultural, family, friendship, environmental, civic, and global. Religious life is lived in response to all these worlds, even in regions where there is no reference to God.[19] In the life of a Christian, God can be present whenever life in this world is lived joyfully, eagerly, earnestly, bravely—even without any explicit reference to religion. This is true because God wills the world, precisely in its worldliness and as a world made by men and women themselves, a secular world. Today men and women experience the world more as their own. God has let the world today grow

---

[17]John Zizioulas offers an image of God's own heart which models the basis of religious life. He interprets *Genesis* as depicting God freely choosing to create all that exists and choosing to be present to it in a providential manner. "The world then is a product of freedom (rather than of necessity), and it is founded in a living personal relationship with its divine Creator." *Being as Communion: Studies in Personhood and the Church* (Crestwood, NY: St. Vladimir's Seminary Press, 1985), 41. As quoted in Mary Frohlich, *Breathed into Wholeness*, 126. See Also: Judith A. Merkle, *Committed by Choice* (Collegeville, MN: The Liturgical Press, 1993).
[18]Karl Rahner, "The Certainty of Faith," in *The Practice of Faith: A Handbook of Contemporary Spirituality* (New York: Crossroad, 1983), 42. We say this with recognition of those with a contemplative calling as one in which intercession for the needs of the world is at its core.
[19]For reflection on how the context of these different worlds impact the Christian life see: Merkle, *Being Faithful*, op. cit.

immeasurably, compared with the worlds of earlier ages. Despite all its ills, God has let the world grow and flourish. It is no longer true that the world only becomes human when people make it so in forms of communal worship and religious poetry, or in ascribing an explicitly religious meaning to it and using it in explicitly religious ways. "Whenever secular life is lived with unreserved honesty there *ipso facto* an essential element in religious life is already present because God loves the world in itself, endows it with grace in itself and in no sense regards it as a rival to himself as though he were envious of it."[20]

The community of believers can find themselves at odds with this world and can dissociate themselves from the current feelings and opinions of their social environment. They can express their faith in and through a critical attitude to their society and its ruling forces.[21] A faith community can challenge the hegemony of the state and the market as the sole determiners of our global future. They can affirm the dignity of the person in terms other than their monetary value. They can protest war, poverty, racist practices, environmental destruction, and increasing threats to democracy across the world. We have noted that the cohesiveness of the Christian life is not that it creates a separate culture with uniform behavior, but that it provides an abiding reference point for the direction of one's life, both in and out of the Christian community. Cultural identity of Christians today is a hybrid, where gospel ideals are lived out in relationships of resistance, appropriation, subversion, and compromise.[22] Religious congregations have at the heart of their life and mission the call to respond to these issues which they share with all people, according to their charism and resources, and as an expression of their core religious commitment.

Religious life can be expressed in the secular world because one who engages this world with genuine love, ipso facto, encounters in it the Cross of Christ and the inconceivability of God, according to Rahner. He or she has no need to conjure up these fingerprints of God

---

[20]Karl Rahner, "Christian Living Formerly and Today," in *Theological Investigations VII*, trans. David Bourke (New York: The Seabury Press, 1971), 17.
[21]Rahner, "The Situation of Faith Today," 31.
[22]Kathryn Tanner, *Theories of Culture: A New Agenda for Theology* (Minneapolis, MN: Fortress Press, 1997), 25–9, 58, 98.

first for them to be present there. Nor do religious or any other member of the church need to pretend they totally understand the world, nor have the clarity about all its dimensions This posture of the church, and in part of congregations, belonged to a church long ago and seemed necessary to assert its place in a world that tended to dismiss it.[23] When Vatican II shifted from an institutional to a theological understanding of the church, the role of social ministries in religious life took on new meaning. When the church is seen in its religious nature as a sacrament, its work for justice is also reinterpreted. The social mission is no longer one of the tasks that the institution (or the religious congregation) performs. Instead, the social mission is a symbol and sacrament of the religious nature of the church. Religious life itself takes on a "sacramental" identity in the church and the world—not as one of the seven sacraments, but religious by public profession participate in the social mission as well as the religious nature of the church.

Religious who search in faith with all people of goodwill neither dismiss the religious significance of matters of everyday life nor take a stance that we know everything, have understood everything, and have an explanation that covers all matters of this world and human relationships. Rather, religious are men and women who practice the virtues of the world, who suffer themselves to be educated by it in joyfulness, courage, devotion to duty, and love. When they do so they are practicing a vital element in genuine religion and these virtues, which can appear worldly, will also serve to open to them the innermost mystery which they contain, namely God's own self. Whatever in the human person is really of value and fundamentally alive is already summoned to receive the grace of Christ even before it is explicitly "baptized." Religious contribute to this human pursuit the conviction that no one is the achiever of his or her own integrity; God alone always remains the true center at the heart of every human journey—whether this is explicitly known or not.[24]

Religious life is a response to this encounter with ". . . the Cross of Christ and the inconceivability of God" which is already in

---

[23]Brian Hehir, "The Social Role of the Church: Leo XIII, Vatican II and John Paul II," in *Catholic Social Thought and the New World Order*, ed. Oliver F. Williams, C.S.C. and John Houck (Notre Dame, IN: University of Notre Dame Press, 1993), 33.
[24]Rahner, "Christian Living Formerly and Today," 16–19.

the world and confronts every human being who lives in it. The contemporary desire to separate from the evil and suffering of the world and to anchor in the good is expressed by religious through their witness to the paschal mystery.[25] It is not the world in which the religious lives which distinguish them, but the means they take to flourish in this world, a world which they share with all human beings and creation itself. Not everyone responds to the Cross of Christ and the inconceivability of God in the same way, yet their answer is their response to the call of salvation and to the call of conscience. This summons is a universal truth of every life. This is the call to live rightly, to choose between right and wrong, and to adopt a life of virtue within the framework of a life course.

Markers of Faith

Faith is the positive and unconditional acceptance of one's own existence as meaningful and open to final fulfillment which we call God.[26] Religious witness publicly to this call of faith through their vows. When we seek confirmation of this stance through the measure of former accomplishments, doubt festers. Institutions which once and may still serve the needs of others and witness to the presence of God—schools, hospitals, networks of advocacy, aid, and care of the elderly—are certainly necessary for the work of the church. However, the role of religious in them has changed. Alone, they cannot be measures of the identity and success of religious life. The "certainty" of belonging to a congregation of such and such a size, running numerous institutions, having this many new entrants each year, does mirror a commonsense assessment of former times— we must be doing the right thing since we are growing. But it does not bring the certainty of faith. The reality to which faith responds is never a particular item of reality, like a school, a ministry, a promotion, or growth in membership—as significant as these can be. Faith responds to the whole of reality in general and to the meaningfulness of human existence. In the words of Michael Paul Gallagher, to find faith today, "people need to discover their souls

---

[25]Taylor, *A Secular Age*, 680–5.
[26]Rahner, "The Certainty of Faith," 32.

first, to retrieve the desires that a dominant lifestyle can smother."[27]
For religious this means continued investment in spiritual renewal.

How Do We Know?

Certainty in life about the worth of important matters comes not simply through one's head but through one's heart. The ability to ground life on a firm foundation is a central challenge of faith. Maurice Blondel charges that we can go a long time living on the surface with the movements of our interior life unnoticed. This can be true of religious as responsibilities in ministry focus their energies on the hustle and bustle of the here and now. We can be unaware of the distance between our hopes and achievements, the contradictions in our lives, or that anything is lacking. Yet there can be a change.[28] Life can call us to reconnect to a deeper life. In 1961 Dag Hammarskjold, then secretary general of the United Nations, wrote in his spiritual diary, later published as *Markings*: "at some moment I did answer Yes to Someone—or Something—and from that hour I was certain that existence is meaningful and that, therefore, my life, in self-surrender had a goal."[29] At many junctures of religious life, whatever measure we used for success is challenged, and the deeper question arises: what is the path on which Christ is leading me? Blondel holds that action to move forward brings a new threshold of religious meaning. From generosity, toward a challenge which faces us, flows an awareness of God that no philosophical speculation can produce, or no statistical proof can affirm. In generosity of action, we become sharers in what we are not aware of possessing. We unite with God in a new way. Certain realities only show themselves to us as real when we entrust ourselves to them and freely choose them. Selfless love, therefore, is only discovered by choosing it. Without the trust of believing, the conversation regarding the worth of faith is only theoretical. Sociologist Hans Joas does not see religious faith as based on utility, or on the calculation of the affinities or advantages of selecting one choice over another. In his words: "It

---

[27]Michael Paul Gallagher, S.J., *Faith Maps* (New York: Paulist Press, 2010), 4.
[28]Maurice Blondel, *Action: Essay on a Critique of Life and a Science of Practice (1893)* (Notre Dame, IN: University of Notre Dame Press, 1984), 330–4.
[29]As quoted in Gallagher, *Faith Maps*, 29.

is phenomenologically inadequate to classify the actual experience constitutive of religious faith as a choice."[30] When one is deeply moved or seized by something, one experiences self-surrender. Something new happens which a former conceptual framework does not hold. A leap of faith transforms us and our understanding, and leads to greater familiarity with the desirable, beyond previous desires.[31] The willingness to follow, to surrender oneself, forms a type of deep values or "data" which become standards by which we evaluate our future preferences. They are emotionally-laden ideas of the desirable rather than desires as such.[32] You become what you love. To witness to what matters, the values of the Kingdom, religious throughout their lives make these surrenders. In fact, it is likely all those in the church who truly love will find their own story in this image.

Hope before Uncertainty: Points of Contacts with the Transcendent/Fullness

Pope Francis, in *Laudato Si'* and *Fratelli Tutti*, calls the church and the world to recognize that not only the care of the earth but the future of the history of the world is entrusted to the whole of humankind (LS 200). The recent pandemic reinforced that no one is saved alone (FT 54). God's covenant and the truth of revealed morality is not just with some of us, set apart, it is with the whole human race. Our future is not ensured within the straitjacket of any nation's security complex; rather, the interdependence of all, as the fact that "everything is connected" forms the ground of a corollary reality—the need for a shared realism about the care of the earth, the geopolitical stability of the world, and the future of humankind.

The virtue of hope may appear to contradict this vision of life. Talking about hope can give the impression that absolute things

---

[30]Joas, *Do We Need Religion?* 29.
[31]Denise Lardner Carmody, "The Desire for Transcendence: Religious Conversion," in *The Desires of the Human Heart: An Introduction to the Theology of Bernard Lonergan*, ed. Vernon Gregson (New York: Paulist Press, 1988), 57–73.
[32]Joas, *Do We Need Religion?* 29. Rahner uses the term "transcendental" to refer to what we live implicitly without putting it into words.

alone, not the negotiations, treaties, policies, and solidarity across the globe, meet the needs of our times. Traditionally, hope is the theological virtue which instills in us the "taste" for God, not just God's gifts. It stirs in us the expectation we can be united with God's own self as we live on this earth and in heaven. The language of the next life seems far from the hope we need to know God in the here and now, and even more distant from the hope we need for the future of our world. Hope helps us believe God makes Godself known to us through the world. Pope Francis reminds us, "Hope is bold; it can look beyond personal convenience, the petty securities and compensations which limit our horizon, and it can open us up to grand ideals that make life more beautiful and worthwhile" (FT 55). When we search as religious congregations to "sense the Spirit," we count on the gift of hope to accomplish it.

Hope and This Life

Hope distinguishes the Christian life from the world of exclusive humanism. Believers share with others the desire to improve the world—to see our projects and plans come to fruition. It is human to want to make things better in the increments of planning with which we are familiar. Disappointment enters when we sense that our frame of the future is not going to happen. Our successes and failures can open us to our need of God and of the gift of hope. Rahner reminds us that hope, ". . . forbids us to invent our own happiness and struggle for the paradise we like. It jars us out of all our life's evidences, plausibilities, and comfortable securities, and shoves us into the infinite darkness of God, which we can really only behold with God's eyes."[33] Yet hope is centered in the belief that humans are both grounded and graced. Religious life expresses a vision of the human person who is not only a creature of God but a partner with God. Grounding in God is at the core of one's integrity, the function of conscience, and one's capacity to respond to the gift of hope.

---

[33]Karl Rahner, "Hope," in *The Practice of Faith: A Handbook of Contemporary Spirituality* (New York: Crossroad, 1983), 249.

Hope is not just an activity of the heart or mind; it is only possessed through practice. We express our hopes in concrete investments in the matters of this world. Hope is what enables us to continually invest in what might seem discouraging. Hope grounds the capacity to make a plan which is not perfect but serves an immediate need. We cannot rid the world of hunger but can supply this soup kitchen. No political party, organization of a diocese or congregation, government plan, or project of social reform is final. A concrete form of Christian hope is the courage of self-commitment to the incalculable and uncontrollable, with the will to accomplish the provisional and needed.

Hope certainly has been required in the flux of our times. Those in leadership facing pandemics, scandals in the church, war, climate upheaval, and economic ups and downs have had to give more attention to the unplanned than the planned. Planning simply highlights the presence of the unplanned which often supersedes it. Some congregations, through their planning, reach the conclusion that their mission has come to completion. This is not a decision without hope. It is an affirmation that the absolute hope which called them together remains present among them as they take responsibility for each other and their patrimony. Their decision is grounded in the facticity of this world and a surrender to the incalculable and uncontrollable which transcends self and their own time. God is always in reality, and this reality is also one which can be acknowledged in hope.

However, if the absolute hope we have for the future gets collapsed into our plan as the absolute plan, then we engage in a "form of presumption which only recognizes that which can be controlled and manipulated, or which treats that which is not subject to our control or calculations as though it were so."[34] This feeds despair, a state in which nothing more is hoped for, and everything is negated. Even the changes in congregations at the time of Vatican II can become old, petrified, and empty. A realistic hope acknowledges even good plans are not those of the absolute future. Hope calls us to recognize God calling us forward, with the recognition we are stewards of these moments of our congregation's pilgrimage with the People of God.

---

[34]Ibid., 259.

Toward a True Secularity

One factor that contributes to uncertainty in religious congregations before secular society is that congregations no longer participate, in the same ways as before, in the creation of parallel ecclesial institutions. The absence of familiar institutional patterns can contribute to ambiguity as to appropriate ways to express belief publicly, and when to do so. Some individuals conclude the best way to proceed is to sever faith from professional, political, and cultural activities. In this thinking, the service provided by religious to others exhausts the meaning of their lives and contribution. The need for religious reference to express their life and mission may appear unnecessary or unwise. Patricia Wittberg mentions that the absence of an ideological framework in religious life in new times opens the door for other sources to fill the vacuum. This creates "boundary-spanning" ties. Membership in professional secular associations and employment in increasingly bureaucratized organizational settings can spark invidious comparisons that place their religious order in an inferior position in the lives of some religious. The importance of a religious community to continue to influence the identity of its members in a positive way is challenged by the fact the life meaning of members has been engulfed by the larger social structure.[35] The tension between the acknowledgment of God in a secular setting and the option to abandon any public religious identity is a difficult one to manage.[36] When language as well as experiences to affirm religious identity alongside societal/professional investment is lacking in a congregational setting, members may wonder where they fit in. It is a tension that both the member and the congregation must work to resolve. When this does not occur, there is a turn to

---

[35]Patricia Wittberg, *From Piety to Professionalism and Back: Transformations of Organized Religious Virtuosity* (Lanham, MD: Lexington Books, 2006), 263–4.

[36]Membership in professional associations have been a lifeline for religious especially if they have been prepared in ministry areas not shared by many in their congregation. Their positive contribution to these associations is also a form of their ministry. However, the integration of the worlds of profession and congregation can be a challenge unless there is a consciousness of the importance of both worlds on the part of the member as well as the congregation.

a type of progressivism where one response to secular society is simply to let one's Christian identity evaporate.[37]

Another posture of uncertainty before secular society is the attitude that the church and the congregation already have the answers to a fulfilled life in secular times, and there is no need for input from or dialogue with the society at large. There is no common search to integrate faith and the secular with others worth taking, as the answers already exist within. Membership in the congregation is to step away from secularity toward another world. The congregation itself offers, amid the metaphysical and existential uncertainties of secular time, a home for the mind and spirit. Members are simply to consign their identity to this ready-made synthesis.

This posture is not just an interpretation of life found in the church and in some congregations—it is also modeled in society. One party, ideological system, racial theory, and television network, offers the same over-arching promise. Accept it and suddenly what has become dark and anxious becomes clear, just as accepted standards of racism, sexism, and classism undermine people's ability to think and feel, thus dimming the public vision of a wider public good. The religious version of these conceptual attitudes offers an answer to uncertainty which fits all complexity into one mental system. This posture mirrors a deep uncertainty as to how to uncover the meaning of the gospel in secular culture, and can be carried out without reliance on the gift of hope. John Paul II claims that both a sense of transcendence and compenetration are needed to witness the gospel in our times.[38] To locate all truth in one system does not affirm God's wisdom: it obscures it. As theologian Shawn Copeland would put it: "If the real is equated with the visible, then the invisible becomes culturally incredible."[39] Pope Francis sees the need for community as necessary to foster an alternate posture:

No one can face life in isolation . . .. We need a community that support and helps us, in which we can help one another to

---

[37]See: Frederick Christian Bauerschmidt, "After Christendom: Catholicism in a More Secular Future," *Commonweal*, May 19, 2022.

[38]John Paul II speaks about the need for a sense of transcendence and compenetration to accomplish this in society. See: Merkle, *From the Heart of the Church: The Catholic Social Tradition*, 236.

[39]Shawn Copeland as quoted in Michael Paul Gallagher, *Faith Maps: Ten Religious Explorers from Newman to Joseph Ratzinger* (New York: Paulist Press, 2010), 69.

keep looking ahead. How important it is to dream together . . ..
By ourselves, we risk seeing mirages, things that are not there.
dreams on the other hand, are built together. Let us dream, then,
as a single human family, as fellow travelers sharing the same
flesh, as children of the same earth, which is our home. Each of
us bringing the richness of his or her beliefs and convictions, each
of us with his or her own voice, brothers and sisters all. (FT 7)

The church and the congregation provide a framework in the
life of a religious, yet this does not provide a ready-made life. The
authenticity of life and the development of conscience also must occur.
A type of individuality, one's own integrity, is essential in religious
life; it is the first response to the essential vocation given by God to
each human being, becoming yourself. Hope embraces the possibility
of this authenticity in God's love. False approaches to secularity as
all-encompassing thought systems, religious or nonreligious, liberal
or conservative, are simply an evasion and shortcut to this process,
and one that cannot serve over the long haul. It is for the long haul in
the complexity of life for which hope is given as a gift.

Discernment is the only path to an openness to God's Spirit. The
Spirit of God is one who directs the unfolding of time and renews
the face of the earth. This is the God who is never absent from
all levels of development. This is the God who takes seriously our
plans, as part of God's ongoing plan. This is the God who gives us
hope. Without a life of prayer and commitment to the spiritual life,
discernment is a term that just covers up decisions made by other
standards alone. Hope before the uncertainty of our times will lead
us to find ways to "give reason for our hope" before the world today.
The Spirit in this case becomes a reality in the story of a religious
and one's congregation, in the Spirit's role of guiding both in hope,
and in making decisions before the uncertainty which confronts
them. The gift of hope is there to strengthen their belonging to Jesus
and to know their next steps in sharing his mission.

Love before Fear: Giving an Answer
to Evil and Suffering in a New Age

The question posed to Jesus about the great commandment was
a question about meaning, value, and fulfillment. When people

asked what the greatest commandment was, they were questioning, how are we to love? Today we ponder Jesus' response in a climate where the preservation of self and pursuit of one's own well-being and pleasure hold center stage in the cultural imagination. Many in society live beyond this sense of narcissism, displaying their strong desire to relieve the suffering of others. Yet they struggle with how to get others to join them. Societally we assume that people will simply be moved by the suffering and pain of others, and nothing more is needed.[40] There is often a denial of the gap in the human heart between these altruistic desires and their contrary. While there is nothing wrong with the view of a good life as the chance to live out one's desires, society makes little distinction between the relative merit of desires or even their conflict with one another. Taylor charges secular society seldom recognizes "strong evaluations": the acknowledgment that certain goals or ends make a claim on us. Nor is there admission that they can be incommensurable with our other desires and purposes. Since such goals require difficult freedom of choice and the capacity to make such choices, they easily can be left unrealized. Eventually even the goal of universal benevolence lacks the moral sources and basis which could support it, in face of conflicting possibilities.

The modern predicament is not one where happiness is made impossible by the demands of religion as once charged by Enlightenment thinkers. The paradox inherent to modern society is one of "maximal demand." Moral aspirations of the modern age carry a heavy sense of moral obligation. In face of the lack of agreement on the moral sources, which underpin these goals, religion is called upon to witness God's love today. We have noted that the type of moral stretch which it takes to repeatedly seek universal justice has been upheld in the West through a belief in *agape*, God's universal love for all. Jesus' great commandment means more than societal ideals uphold. A strong sense that human beings are worth helping or treating with justice, a sense of their dignity or value, is an encounter with moral sources which connect their goodness as creatures to the love God has for them. Religious life has, as its *raison d'etre*, the experience of and witness to this love.

---

[40]Taylor, *The Secular Age*, 331.

Love and Religious Life

It is not that religious life requires a type of universal will, as in kindergarten, to "love" everyone. The choice of Christian celibacy in religious life makes sense only for the sake of love—"or better, for the sake of at least a desire to love God with one's whole heart and soul and mind and strength, and to love one's neighbor as oneself."[41] It is not the case that religious forego all human interpersonal intimacy, experiences we normally understand as love. Friendships without genital content, love of family, and deep spiritual connections with others throughout their lifetime, offer an intimacy sometimes beyond that of the sexually partnered. Central to the commitment of celibacy is a letting go of sexual and marital intimacy, as well as the establishment of a family, not the letting go of love. The expression of celibacy of a religious is a response to a perceived call; the reasons for its renunciations are centered in the love of God and the People of God. Both provide lifelong possibilities for relationships and intimacy with others in community, ministry, and shared endeavors. Religious do not will this love as if it is a fruit of their moral effort alone. Nor are they the only people who express it, as all love requires sacrifice and commitment. Religious, however, participate in the mystery of God's love through their efforts to learn to love as do all in the church. Through their vows, religious mark their embodied identity as adult Christians, as one characterized by both grace and love or charity. When a religious accounts for a lifetime of service and love which the course of their lives unfolds, they cannot help but uncover the energy and mystery of how God has worked in them and through them in countless ways. The children, men, and women whom neither tribe, nor family, nor nation or choice alone has put into their lives have been touched by God's love through their lives and they touched through others. The central energy of religious life is not willpower, but love. It is not the case that religious are perfect in their love, as is the human condition. "The central rationale for this life may be found, finally in the desire to pick up one's own very being and place it down against in utter affirmation of God; and in doing so, in profound

---

[41]Margaret A. Farley, "Celibacy Under the Sign of the Cross," in *Changing the Questions*, ed. Jamie L. Manson (New York: Maryknoll, 2015), 239.

love of and solidarity with the neighbor near and far."[42] This love
empowers the lives of religious and remains the mystery and door
to union with God and others.

Fullness and Love in Religious Life

At its heart, the distinctive lifestyle of religious life in a secular world
is embedded in love and its meaning.[43] Defining a "life" course
requires reasons which are trustworthy. There must be an inner
cohesion which links a sense of purpose and self-understanding to
meaningful activities in ordinary life. The two need to overlap in
real time and space, in life choices which have significance both
now and in relation to ultimate matters. The significance of religious
life rests in the love which defines it, the grace and happiness it
brings to those who live it, and the fruits it offers to the church and
society. Today the exact patterns of how religious life will emerge as
a lifestyle in the future is unclear. Yet there are some markers which
point to its distinctive nature. One, religious life has at its core a
religious motivation, love of God and others. There is a timelessness
in this core intention to love, even though varied life goals and
fulfillments are involved in the choice of religious life. Attention to
God affects the entire horizon of experience in the life of a religious
as it impacts values, meaning, and a sense of fullness. It serves to
organize and prioritize for a religious the many dimensions of his
or her life: patterns of collaboration, use of money, homes, use of
talents, and relationships. It helps them walk the journey of their
own integration and face the issues which arise in each person's
struggle for authenticity. It stabilizes them through the inescapable
routine and ordinariness of daily living, as well as the inevitable
disappointments and struggles of a life course. It is possible that a
person can join a congregation yet never embark on the spiritual
journey this love entails. However, this prevents them from the
fulfillment religious life can offer, as well as the satisfaction of
other paths. Second, the charism of a religious congregation offers

---

[42]Ibid., 240.
[43]See: Judith A. Merkle, *A Different Touch: A Study of the Vows in Religious Life*
(Collegeville, MN: The Liturgical Press, 1998).

an intentional structure which impacts choice and deliberations across a lifetime. A religious unites his or her own intention to love with this value-laden broader structure of community. Beyond the modern dilemmas of "feeling used" (instrumentalism) or myopic self-fulfillment (individualism) charism sharpens and focuses one's moral perspective of the higher good and offers significance to the choices along the way. Third, the experience of God is everywhere for the Christian, but for each person, it also needs to be somewhere. Charism and community provide a map which helps to shape, not only the changing aspirations of a religious and congregation, but to clarify what is important over time in new situations.

The shape of religious community of the future is not clear. The parochial, geographically-limited, and culturally-singular patterns of nineteenth-century communities will likely not be the paradigm of the future. However, religious life cannot be just everything. A desire for "fullness," which orients us morally or spiritually, contains a drive to align it with some form of lifestyle.[44] The transformative union of the human person with God and others is the life of grace in religious life.

This grace helps a religious become more and more who they really are as a person, live more in union with Jesus Christ, and consciously be one with creation, their neighbor, and the processes of their world at the time. The organization of a religious lifestyle across the centuries had the same intention as the work of the Holy Spirit. It was not the only way, but one way, to help seeking Christians to understand, express, and cooperate with grace in their lives.[45] It seems reasonable to hold that, while the future of religious life is unlikely to be what we know today, it will not be a free-floating lifestyle without the characteristics of an adult form of living which has characterized vocations in the church throughout the centuries.

Religious life as a vocation is a path to strengthen our desire to love God in all we do. In each age, it arises out of a stance of belief, the mentality of the times, the circumstances and challenges of the age, and the aptitudes and gifts of the individuals who form it. Theologian Bernard Lonergan refers to the ongoing process where

---

[44]Taylor, A Secular Age, 6.
[45]See: Merkle, Beyond Our Lights and Shadows, 3–27.

the love of God integrates all these factors as religious conversion—one related to other conversions but not identical to them. It seems to be a safe assumption that the centrality of religious conversion is a key characteristic of religious life today and in the future.

Love and Conversion

For Lonergan, falling in love with God, without limits or qualifications or conditions or reservations, is the proper fulfillment of the human person's unrestricted capacity for self-transcendence.[46] Amid our questions, personal gifts, and accomplishments in life, which draw on our capacities to experience, understand, judge, and decide, we seek something beyond them: we seek more. The human spirit is oriented to ask, not just about the particulars of a situation, but the whole or ground behind it; this is the question of God. Religious life is different from the goodwill expressed in forms of exclusive humanism. It offers a public witness to and consciousness of God as a mystery who changes one's life. Through its capacity to be total, the love expressed in religious conversion has the potential to open new horizons, make a difference, and be the impetus of "breakthrough" to new meaning.

In Lonergan's understanding of the inner workings of the human person, the experience of religious conversion is not the same as the conversions experienced at prior levels of consciousness. The pursuit of what is of ultimate value fulfills all the intentional desires the person sought consciously in previous ways. The fourth level of consciousness, religious conversion, involves an unrestricted orientation to "know and do, not just what pleases us," but what is truly good, worthwhile and to "be principles of benevolence and beneficence, capable of genuine collaboration and of true love."[47] For Lonergan, being in love in an unrestricted manner is a share in God's own life.

Through this transformation of a person (and a congregation) there is the animation of community at a familial, social, cultural,

---

[46]Lonergan, *Method in Theology*, 105–6.
[47]Lonergan, *Method in Theology*, 35. See also: Robert Doran, "Discernment and Lonergan's Fourth Level of Consciousness," *Gregorianum* 89, no. 4 (2008): 290–302.

ecclesial, and global level. Bias and dysfunction, especially motivated by fear, can block the impetus toward authentic living at all levels of life. To the degree that individuals and groups are willing to walk the path of human and spiritual conversion there exists the possibility that real transformation of these realms can occur. Religious congregations can challenge the ideologies and patterns of conduct which maintain these systems which inhibit human flourishing. Together people can merge their gifts and talents through solidarity in the mission, to bring a prophetic voice to the church and the world.

Love Which Casts out Fear: Facing Evil and Suffering

Religious life is not a flight from this world and its challenges; it is an immersion in love, and in the life and future shared by humankind. The love which grounds religious life is not a love of God as a personal achievement. Rather it is one where one disposes oneself to God and opens to God's love. This love is grace and is relied on in face of the cross. The manifestations of personal sin met on the journey—the evil and suffering of war and racism, misunderstanding, alienation, and selfishness in church and community—are met in union with God's abiding love, despite the struggle. The struggle is the vocation. Religious commitment involves a love of neighbor which is more than a commandment of loving God. Over time the religious learns it is the love God has for us that makes the love of neighbor possible.[48]

In society, people often do not see that love of God is necessary for love of neighbor, however, believers see things differently.[49] There is no love for God that is not, in itself, a love of neighbor; and love for God only comes to fulfillment in a love for neighbor. Only one who loves his or her neighbor can even know who God is. As Christians, and as religious, we love Jesus concretely and intimately, as we would love a friend, even across the historical

---

[48]Karl Rahner, "Love of God and Human Beings," in *The Practice of Faith: A Handbook of Contemporary Spirituality* (New York: Crossroad, 1983), 136.
[49]Merkle, *Discipleship, Secularity and the Modern Self*, 201.

divide between his life and ours. Love of God, whether we are conscious of it or not, grounds the unconditional love of another person which challenges us every day and helps us move beyond the limitations which prevent it.

Religious life is not the only lifestyle in which religious conversion has a central role; however, without it, religious life is not sustainable. The faith, hope, and love which are central to religious life are contested today by new pressures. While we experience in our modern age vast resources to create the new patterns needed for the future, we recognize as religious that, as with the ice plants in the desert, it might be our "reserves" that are invaluable for what is yet to come. The ultimate explanation, final sense-making, and witness of spiritual transformation of those who have gone before us is witnessed as a deep and confident sign—there is a way ahead. God will enable in us the freedom to recreate manifestations in this world of the sacred calling which has always sustained the commitment of religious life. For the rest of us, we pray to "sense the Spirit" responsibly, amid the chaotic flux of our times. We ask for the grace of trust to move forward—for the sake of those who will follow and for the life of the church and the world.

BIBLIOGRAPHY

Ahern, Kevin. "Rejoice and be Glad." *America*, April 30, 2019.

Alfaro, Juan. "Faith." In *Sacramentum Mundi*, edited by Karl Rahner, Vol. 2. London: Burns and Oates, 1968.

Allsopp, Michael E. "Principle of Subsidiarity." In *The New Dictionary of Catholic Social Thought*, edited by Judith A. Dwyer, 927–9. Collegeville, MN: Liturgical Press, 1994.

Annett, Anthony. "The Economic Vision of Pope Francis." In *The Theological and Ecological Vision of Laudato Si'*, edited by Vincent Miller, 165–85. London: Bloomsbury/T&T Clark, 2017.

Aschenbrenner, George, S.J. "A Consoling Companion, Faithful Beyond Any Doubt." *The Way* 46, no. 3 (July 2007): 67–83.

Augustine of Hippo. *The City of God*. Translated by Marcus Dodds. New York: Random House, 1950.

Aumann, Jordan. *Spiritual Theology*. London: Sheed and Ward, 1990.

Bauerschmidt, Frederick Christian. "After Christendom: Catholicism in a More Secular Future." *Commonweal*, May 19, 2022.

Bauman, Zygmunt. *Liquid Modernity*. Cambridge, MA: Polity Press, 2000.

Bellah, Robert et al. *Habits of the Heart: Individualism and Commitment in American Life*. Berkley, CA: University of California Press, 1985.

Bettencourt, Estevao. "Charism." In *Sacramentum Mundi*, edited by Karl Rahner et al., Vol. 1, 233–4. New York: Herder and Herder, 1968.

Bisson, Peter, S.J. "The Post-Conciliar Jesuit Congregations: Social Commitment Constructing a New World of Religious Meaning." *Lonergan Workshop* 19 (2007): 1–35.

Blake, John. "An Imposter Christianity is Threatening American Democracy." *CNN*, July 24, 2022.

Blondel, Maurice. *Action: Essay on a Critique of Life and a Science of Practice (1893)*. Notre Dame, IN: University of Notre Dame Press, 1984.

Boyle, Joseph. "Natural Law." In *The New Dictionary of Theology*, edited by Joseph A. Komonchak, Mary Collins and Dermot A. Lane, 703–8. Collegeville, MN: The Liturgical Press, 1987.

Brink, Laurie, O.P. *The Heavens Are Telling the Glory of God: An
    Emerging Chapter for Religious Life. Science, Theology and Mission.*
    Collegeville, MN: Liturgical Press, 2022.
Brown, Peter. *The Body and Society: Men, Women and Sexual Renunciation
    in Early Christianity.* New York: Columbia University Press, 1988.
Browning, Don D. *Marriage and Modernization: How Globalization
    Threatens Marriage and What to Do About It.* Grand Rapids, MI:
    Eerdmans, 2003.
Burke, Kevin. "Love Will Decide Everything: Pedro Arrupe Recovered the
    Ignatian 'Mysticism of Open Eyes.'" *America*, November 12, 2007.
Cahill, Edward, S.J. "The Catholic Movement: Historical Aspects." In
    Readings in Moral Theology, No. 5 Official Catholic Social Teaching,
    edited by Richard A. McCormick, 3–31. New York: Paulist Press, 1986.
Cahill, Lisa Sowle. "Notes on Moral Theology: Marriage: Developments in
    Catholic Theology and Ethics." *Theological Studies* 64 (2003): 95–100.
Cantwell, Peter. "Why Newly Professed Leave." *Review for Religious* 62
    (2003): 379–401.
Carmody, Denise Lardner. "The Desire for Transcendence: Religious
    Conversion." In *The Desires of the Human Heart: An Introduction to
    the Theology of Bernard Lonergan,* edited by Vernon Gregson, 57–73.
    New York: Paulist Press, 1988.
Carroll, Anthony J., S.J. *Weber, Secularization, and Protestantism.*
    Scranton and London: The University of Scranton Press, 2007.
Carter, Stephen L. *Civility, Manners, Morals and the Etiquette of
    Democracy.* New York: Harper Collins, 1998.
Casanova, Jose. *Public Religions in the Modern World.* Chicago, IL: The
    University of Chicago Press, 1994.
Casanova, Jose. "The Contemporary Disjunction Between Social and
    Church Morality." In *Church and People: Disjunctions in a Secular
    Age,* edited by George F. McLean, 127–35. Washington, DC: The
    Council for Research in Values and Philosophy, 2012.
Catechism of the Catholic Church. Apostolic Constitution *Fidei
    Depositum.* Edited by John Paul II, Bishop. Liguori, MO: Liguori
    Publications, 1994.
Chauvet, Louis-Marie. *The Sacraments: The Word of God at the Mercy of
    the Body.* Collegeville, MN: The Liturgical Press, 2001.
Chauvet, Louis-Marie. *Symbol and Sacrament: A Sacramental Interpretation
    of Christian Existence.* Collegeville, MN: The Liturgical Press, 1995.
Cimperman, Maria, R.S.C.J. *Religious Life for Our World: Creating
    Communities of Hope.* Maryknoll, NY: Orbis Books, 2020.
Cimperman, Maria, R.S.C.J. and Roger P., S.V.D. Schroeder, eds.
    Engaging Our Diversity: Interculturality and Consecrated Life Today.
    Maryknoll, NY: Orbis Books, 2020.

Coakley, Sara. *The New Asceticism: Sexuality, Gender and the Quest for God*. London: Bloomsbury, 2015.

Cone, James. *Speaking the Truth: Ecumenism, Liberation and Black Theology*. Grand Rapids. MI: Eerdmans, 1986.

Confoy, Maryanne, R.S.C. *Religious Life and Priesthood: Rediscovering Vatican II*. New York: Paulist, 2008.

Congar, Yves, O.P. *I Believe in the Holy Spirit: The Complete Three Volume Work in One Volume*. Translated by David Smith. New York: Crossroad, 1983.

Congar, Yves, O.P. *Spirit of God: Short Writings on the Holy Spirit*. Washington, DC: The Catholic University of America Press, 2018.

Curran, Charles. *The Social Mission of the U.S. Catholic Church: A Theological Perspective*. Washington, DC: Georgetown University Press, 2010.

DeCosse, David E. and Thomas A. O.F.M. Nairn, eds. *Conscience and Catholic Health Care: From Clinical Contexts to Government Mandates*. Maryknoll, NY: Orbis, 2017.

Djupe, Paul A. and Laura R. Olson. *Encyclopedia of American Religion and Politics*, 148. Facts on File Library of American History Series, 2003.

Doran, Robert, S.J. "From Psychic Conversion to the Dialectic of Community." In *Lonergan Workshop*, edited by Robert C. Croken, Frederick F. Crowe, and Robert M. S.J. Doran, Vol. 6. Toronto: University of Toronto Press, 1990.

Doran, Robert, S.J. "Discernment and Lonergan's Fourth Level of Consciousness." *Gregorianum* 89, no. 4 (2008): 790–802.

Douglas, Mary. *Natural Symbols: Explorations in Cosmology*. New York: Pantheon Books, 1982.

Dowling, Kevin, CSsR. "Revisioning Religious Life for the 21st Century in a Global Context." Annual General Meeting of the Conference of Religious of Ireland, June 4, 2015.

Dumas, Bertrand. "The Sacrament of Marriage in Postmodernity: Struggling with 'Spectacularization.'" *Marriage, Families, and Spirituality* 27, no. 2 (2021): 175–95.

Ehrman, Terrence P., C.S.C. "Ecology: The Science of Interconnections." In *The Theological and Ecological Vision of Laudato Si': Everything is Connected*, edited by Vincent J. Miller, 51–73. London: Bloomsbury/ T&T Clark, 2017.

Farley, Margaret A., R.S.M. "Celibacy Under the Sign of the Cross." In *Changing Questions: Explorations in Christian Ethics*, edited and introduction by Jamie L. Manson. New York: Orbis Books, 2015.

Finn, Daniel. *Christian Economic Ethics*. Minneapolis, MN: Fortress Press, 2013.

Fiorenza, Francis Schussler. "Social Mission of the Church." In *The New Dictionary of Catholic Social Thought*, edited by Judith A. Dwyer, 151–71. Collegeville, MN: The Liturgical Press, 1994.

Ford, David F. *Self and Salvation: Being Transformed*. Cambridge, MA: Cambridge University Press, 2003.

Fowler, James. *Becoming Adult, Becoming Christian: Adult Development and Christian Faith*. San Francisco, CA: Jossey-Bass, 2000.

Fragomeni, Richard N. "Conversion." In *The New Dictionary of Catholic Spirituality*, edited by Michael Downey, 234–7. Collegeville, MN: The Liturgical Press, 1993.

Francis, Pope. *Joy of the Gospel: Evangelii Gaudium*. Washington, DC: United States Conference of Catholic Bishops, 2013.

Francis, Pope. *On Care for Our Common Home, Laudato Si'*. Citta del Vaticana: Libreria Editrice Vaticana, 2015.

Francis, Pope. *On Fraternity and Social Friendship: Fratelli Tutti*. Vatican City: Liberia Editrice Vaticana, 2020.

Francis, Pope. *Post Synodal Apostolic Exhortation: Querida Amazonia*. Vatican City: Liberia Editricc Vaticana, 2020.

Frohlich, Mary, R.S.C.J. *Breathed into Wholeness: Catholicity and Life in the Spirit*. New York: Orbis Books, 2019.

Gallagher, Michael Paul, S.J. *Clashing Symbols: An Introduction to Faith and Culture*. New York: Paulist Press, 2003.

Gallagher, Michael Paul, S.J. *Faith Maps*. Mahweh, NJ: Paulist Press, 2010.

Giddens, Anthony. *Self and Society in the Late Modern Age*. Stanford, CA: Stanford University Press, 1997.

Gilman, Richard. "A Life of Letters." *The New York Times*, March 18, 1979.

Gingles, Dallas. "Narrative." In *T&T Clark Handbook of Christian Ethics*, edited by Tobias Winright, 103–10. London: Bloomsbury/T&T Clark, 2021.

Godzieba, Anthony J. *A Theology of the Presence and Absence of God*. Collegeville, MN: Liturgical Press, 2018.

Gorski, Philip S. and Samuel L. Perry. *The Flag and the Cross: White Christian Nationalism and the Threat to American Democracy*. Oxford: Oxford University Press, 2022.

Gregson, Vernon, ed. *The Desires of the Human Heart: An Introduction to the Theology of Bernard Lonergan*. Mahweh, NJ: Paulist Press, 1989.

Groppe, Elizabeth T. "The Love that Moves the Sun and Stars." In *The Theological and Ecological Vision of Laudato Si': Everything is Connected*, edited by Vincent J. Miller, 77–94. London: Bloomsbury/T&T Clark, 2017.

Gudorf, Christine E. "Mutuality." In *The New Dictionary of Catholic Social Thought*, edited by Judith Dwyer, 654–5. Collegeville, MN: The Liturgical Press, 2004.

Haight, Roger, S.J. *Christian Spirituality for Seekers: Reflections on the Spiritual Exercises of Ignatius Loyola*. New York: Orbis Books, 2012.

Haring, Bernard, CSsR. *Free and Faithful in Christ: Moral Theology for Priests and Laity*. Vol. 1. Mahweh, NJ: The Paulist Press, 1978.

Harrington, M. J., et al. "Origami-Like Unfolding of Hydro-actuated Ice Plant Seed Capsules." *Nature Communications* 2, no. 377 (2011).

Harrington,Wilfred, O.P. "Charism." In *The New Dictionary of Theology*, edited by Joseph A. Komonchak, et al., 180–3. Wilmington, DL: Michael Glazier, 1989.

Haughey, John, S.J. "Charisms: An Ecclesiological Exploration." In *Retrieving Charisms for the 21st Century*, edited by Doris Donnelly, 1–16. Collegeville, MN: The Liturgical Press, 1999.

Haughton, Rosemary. *The Passionate God*. New York: Paulist, 1981.

Hehir, Brian. "The Social Role of the Church: Leo XIII, Vatican II and John Paul II." In *Catholic Social Thought and the New World Order*, edited by Oliver F. Williams, C.S.C. and John Houck. Notre Dame, IN: University of Notre Dame Press, 1993.

Hollenbach, David, S.J. *Humanity in Crisis: Ethical and Religious Responses to Refugees*. Washington, DC: Georgetown University Press, 2019.

Ignatius of Loyola. *The Spiritual Exercises of Saint Ignatius*. Translated by Louis, S.J. Puhl. Chicago, IL: Loyola Press, 1968.

Imbelli, Robert P. "Holy Spirit." In *The New Dictionary of Theology*, edited by Joseph A. Komonchak, et al., 474–89. Wilmington, DL: Michael Glazier, 1989.

Irwin, Kevin. "The Sacramentality of Creation and the Role of Creation in the Liturgy and Sacraments." In *And God Saw That It Was Good: Catholic Theology and the Environment*, edited by Drew Christenson and Walter E. Grazer. Washington, DC: United States Catholic Conference, 1996.

James, William. *The Varieties of Religious Experience*. New York: Penguin, 1982.

Jedin, Hubert. "Pope Benedict XV, Pius XI, and Pius XII." In *History of the Church in the Modern Age*, edited by Hubert Jedin, 3–45. London: Burns and Oates, 1981.

Joas, Hans. *The Creativity of Action*. Edited by Jeremy Gaines and Paul Keast. Chicago, IL: University of Chicago Press, 1996.

Joas, Hans. *The Genesis of Values*. Translated by Gregory Moore. Chicago, IL: The University of Chicago Press, 2000.

Joas, Hans. *Do We Need Religion?* Translated by Alex Skinner. London: Paradigm, 2008.

Joas, Hans. *Faith as an Option: Possible Futures for Christianity*. Translated by Alex Skinner. Stanford, CA: Stanford University Press, 2014.

John, Paul II. *Sources of Renewal: The Implementation of the Second Vatican Council*. London: Collins, 1980.

Johnson, Elizabeth, S.S.J. "Christ Died for Us." In *Abounding in Kindness*. New York: Orbis Books, 2015.

Johnson, Mary, SNDdeN, Mary Gautier and Patricia Wittberg SC, Do, Thu, LHC. *Migration for Mission: International Catholic Sisters in the United States*. New York: Oxford University Press, 2019.

Johnstone, Brian V., CSsR. "Moral Methodology." In *The New Dictionary of Catholic Social Thought*, edited by Judith Dwyer, 597–608. Collegeville, MN: The Liturgical Press, 2004.

Julian of Norwich. *Showings*. Edited by Edmund College and James Walsh. The Classics of Western Spirituality. New York: Paulist Press, 1978.

Kappadakunnel, Matt. "Reframing the Catholic Spectrum into a Polyhedron." *Catholic Outlook*, December 19, 2020.

Kasper, Walter. *The Catholic Church: Nature, Reality and Mission*. London: Bloomsbury, 2015.

Larkin, Ernest E. O.Carm. "Religious Life and Vatican II." *The Sword*, 26 February 1966.

LEST-Leuven Encounters in Systematic Theology. "Sacramental Presence in a Postmodern Context—Fundamental Theological Approaches." http://www.lestconference.com/.

Lohfink, Gerard. *The Forty Parables of Jesus*. Translated by Linda M. Mahoney. Collegeville, MN: The Liturgical Press, 2021.

Lonergan, Bernard, S.J. *Insight*. San Francisco, CA: Harper and Row, 1978.

Lonergan, Bernard, S.J. "The Ongoing Genesis of Methods." In *A Third Collections: Papers by Bernard J. F. Lonergan, S.J.*, edited by Frederick E. Crowe. New York: Paulist Press, 1985.

Lonergan, Bernard, S.J. *Method in Theology*. Toronto: University of Toronto Press, 1990.

Lonergan, Bernard, S.J. "Healing and Creating in History." In *The Lonergan Reader*, edited by Mark D. Morelli and Elizabeth A. Morelli [Murray], 136–8. Toronto: University of Toronto Press, 1997.

Markus, Robert A. *Christianity and the Secular*. Notre Dame, IN: University of Notre Dame Press, 2006.

Marmion, Declan, *A Spirituality of Everyday: A Theological Investigation of the Notion of Spirituality in Karl Rahner*. Westminster, MD: Christian Classics, Inc., 1985.

McBrien, Richard B. "What is the Kingdom of God?" http:www.lovingjustwise.com. Website from the Franciscans and St. Anthony Messenger.

McKenzie, John L., S.J. *The Dictionary of the Bible*. Milwaukee: The Bruce Publishing Co., 1966.

McInroy, Mark. *Balthasar on the Spiritual Senses: Perceiving Splendour.* Oxford and New York: Oxford University Press, 2014.

McLean, George F. "Introduction: Disjunction in the 21st Century." In *Church and People: Disjunctions in a Secular Age.* Washington, DC: The Council for Research in Values and Philosophy, 2012.

Merkle, Judith A., SNDdeN. *Committed by Choice.* Collegeville, MN: The Liturgical Press, 1993.

Merkle, Judith A., SNDdeN. *A Different Touch: A Study of the Vows in Religious Life.* Collegeville, MN: The Liturgical Press, 1998.

Merkle, Judith A., SNDdeN. *From the Heart of the Church: The Catholic Social Tradition.* Collegeville, MN: The Liturgical Press, 2004.

Merkle, Judith A., SNDdeN. *Being Faithful: Christian Commitment in Modern Society.* London: Bloomsbury/T&T Clark, 2010.

Merkle, Judith A., SNDdeN. *Beyond Our Lights and Shadows: Charism and Institution in the Church.* London: Bloomsbury/T&T Clark, 2016.

Merkle, Judith A., SNDdeN. *Discipleship, Secularity and the Modern Self: Dancing to Silent Music.* London: Bloomsbury/T&T Clark, 2020.

Metz, Johann Baptist. *Faith in History and Society.* New York: Seabury Press, 1980.

Miller, Vincent. *Consuming Religion: Christian Faith and Practice in a Consumer Culture.* New York: Continuum, 2004.

Miller, Vincent, ed. *The Theological and Ecological Vision of Laudato Si': Everything is Connected.* London: Bloomsbury/T&T Clark, 2017.

Molinski, Waldemar. "Vow." In *Sacramentum Mundi,* edited by Karl Rahner, Vol. 6, 350–2. New York: Herder and Herder, 1970.

Mudge, Lewis S. *The Church as Moral Community: Ecclesiology and Ethics in the Ecumenical Debate.* New York: Continuum, 1998.

Muldoon, Tim. "Postmodern Spirituality and the Ignatian *Fundamentum.*" *The Way* 44, no. 1 (January, 2005): 85–100.

Nothwehr, Dawn, O.S.F. *Mutuality: A Formal Norm for Christian Social Ethics.* Eugene, OR: Wipf and Stock, 2005.

Nygren, David and Miriam Ukeritis. "Executive Summary of Study on the Future of Religious Orders." *Origins* 22, no. 15 (September 24, 1992): 270.

O'Brien, David. "American Catholic and American Society." In *Catholics and Nuclear War,* edited by Philip J. Murnion, 16–29. London: Geoffrey Chapman, 1983.

O'Connor, Flannery. *A Good Man is Hard to Find and Other Stories.* New York: Houghton Mifflin Harcourt, 1992.

Orsi, Robert. *Thank You Saint Jude: Women's Devotion to the Patron Saint of Hopeless Causes.* New Haven, CT: Yale University Press, 1998.

Pennington, Basil M., O.C.S.O. "Monasticism." In *The New Dictionary of Theology*, edited by Joseph A. Komonchak et al., 670–3. Wilmington, DE: Michael Glazier, 1989.

Pine, Gregory, O.P. "Religious Life as a State of Perfection." *Nova et Vetera*, English Edition 19, no. 4 (2021): 1181–214.

Rabut, Oliver. *L'experience religieuse fondamentale*. Tournai: Castermann, 1968.

Rahner, Karl, S.J. *"Christian Living Formerly and Today."* In *Theological Investigations VII*, translated by David Bourke. New York: The Seabury Press, 1971.

Rahner, Karl, S.J. "The Spirituality of the Church of the Future." In *Theological Investigations*, XX. London: Darton, Longman and Todd, 1981.

Rahner, Karl, S.J. "Reflections on the Unity of the Love of Neighbor and the Love of God." In *Theological Investigations*, Vol. VI, trans. Karl H. and Boniface Kruger. New York: Crossroad, 1982.

Rahner, Karl, S.J. "The Certainty of Faith." In *The Practice of Faith: A Handbook of Contemporary Spirituality*. New York: Crossroad, 1983.

Rahner, Karl, S.J. "The Situation of Faith Today." In *The Practice of Faith: A Handbook of Contemporary Spirituality*. New York: Crossroad, 1983.

Rahner, Karl, S.J. "Fraternal Faith." In *The Practice of Faith: A Handbook of Contemporary Spirituality*. New York: Crossroad, 1983.

Rahner, Karl, S.J. "Hope." In *The Practice of Faith: A Handbook of Contemporary Spirituality*. New York: Crossroad, 1983.

Rahner, Karl, S.J. "Love of God and Human Beings." In *The Practice of Faith: A Handbook of Contemporary Spirituality*. New York: Crossroad, 1983.

Rahner, Karl, S.J. "Experience of the Holy Spirit." In *Theological Investigations*, XVIII. New York: Crossroad, 1983.

Rasmussen, Larry. *Moral Fragments, Moral Community*. Minneapolis, MN: Fortress Press, 1993.

Renewing the Church in a Secular Age: Holistic Dialogue and Kenotic Vision. Pontificia Universita Gregoriana, Rome, March 4–5, 2015. Proceedings: Council for Research in Values and Philosophy, Co-sponsored by the Pontifical Council for Culture.

Rigali, Norbert, S.J. "On Christian Ethics." *Chicago Studies* 10 (1971): 227–47.

Rubio, Julie Hanlon. *Family Ethics: Practices for Christians*. Washington, DC: Georgetown University Press, 2010.

Sachs, John R., S.J. "Holy Spirit in Christian Worship." In *The New Dictionary of Sacramental Worship*, edited by Peter E. Fink, S.J., 529–39. Collegeville, MN: The Liturgical Press, 1990.

Schnieller, Peter. *A Handbook of Inculturation*. New York: Paulist, 1990.

Scott, Margaret. "Greening the Vows: *Laudato Si* and Religious Life." *The Way* 54, no. 4 (October 2015): 83–93.

Segundo, Juan Luis. *Faith and Ideologies*. Translated by John Drury. New York: Orbis, 1984.

Selznick, Philip. *The Moral Commonwealth, Social Theory and the Promise of Community*. Berkeley, CA: University of California Press, 1992.

Smith, James K.A. *How (Not) To Be Secular: Reading Charles Taylor*. Grand Rapids, MI: William B. Eerdmans Publishing Company, 2014.

Steck, Christopher, S.J. *The Ethical Thought of Hans Urs von Balthasar*. New York: Crossroads, 2001.

Tanner, Kathryn. *Theories of Culture: A New Agenda for Theology*. Minneapolis, MN: Fortress Press, 1997.

Taylor, Charles. *The Ethics of Authenticity*. Cambridge, MA: Harvard University Press, 1991.

Taylor, Charles. *A Secular Age*. Cambridge, MA: The Belknap Press of Harvard University Press, 2007.

Taylor, Charles. "Disenchantment-Reenchantment." In *Dilemmas and Connections: Selected Essays*, 287–302. Cambridge, MA: The Belknap Press of Harvard University, 2011.

Tillard, J.M.R., O.P. *Flesh of the Church, Flesh of Christ: At the Source of the Ecclesiology of Communion*. Collegeville, MN: The Liturgical Press, 2001.

Ulanov, Ann and Barry Ulanov. *Primary Speech: A Psychology of Prayer*. Louisville, KY: Westminster John Knox Press, 1982.

Ulanov, Ann and Barry Ulanov. *Spiritual Aspects of Clinical Work*. Einsiedeln: Daimon Verlag, 2004.

Vanhoye, Albert, S.J. "The Biblical Question of '*Charisms*' after Vatican II." In *Vatican II: Assessment and Perspectives: Twenty-Five Years After (1962–1987)*, Vol. 1, edited by Rene Latourelle, 439–68. Mahwah, NJ: Paulist Press, 1988.

von Balthasar, Hans Urs. *Elucidations*. Translated by John Riches. San Francisco, CA: Ignatius Press, 1998.

Weber, Max. *On Charism and Institution Building: Selected Papers*. Edited and introduction by S. N. Eisenstadt. Chicago, IL: University of Chicago Press, 1988.

Will, Herberg. *Protestant, Catholic, Jew: An Essay in American Religious Sociology*. Garden City, NY: Doubleday, 1955.

Wittberg, Patricia, S.C. *From Piety to Professionalism and Back? Transformations of Organized Religious Virtuosity*. Lanham, MD: Lexington Books, 2006.

Wooden, Cindy. "Pope Francis Announces Major Overhaul of Roman
      Curia." *Catholic News Service*, March 19, 2022.
Zizioulas, John. *Being as Communion: Studies in Personhood and the
      Church*. Crestwood, NY: St. Vladimir's Seminary Press, 1985.

INDEX

love 159ff
agape 160
religious life and
community 160–5

McBrien, Richard B. 24, 120
McInroy, Mark 131
McKenzie, John 26
Markus, Robert A. 61
Marmion, Declan 73
marriage 114–15, 117
Merkle, Judith 2, 14, 16, 19, 23,
24, 28, 32, 40, 42, 27,
53, 55, 63, 65, 74, 75,
79, 82, 84, 98, 119, 121,
122, 136, 143–5, 149,
158, 162, 165
Miller, Vincent 68, 137
mission 43, 80–1, 99, 107, 112,
150, 165
Molinski, Waldemar 100
moralism 83
Mudge, Lewis 75, 125
Muldon, Tim 105
mysticism 105

Nothwehr, Dawn 55
Nygren, David 45

O'Brien, David 45
O'Connor, Flannery 142, 144–5
Olson, Laura 44
Orsi, Robert 132

Pelagianism 123ff
Pennington, Basil M. 36, 38
Perry, Samuel 80, 122
Pine, Gregory 148
postmodern 21
prayer 69, 159

Rahner, Karl 23, 30, 88, 97–8, 105,
110, 146, 148–52, 155, 165

Rasmussen, Larry 53
religious desire 68–70
religious life
context 33–4
culture 45–50, 150
bundling-unbundling 49
interculturality 56, 133
elements
bridge between church and
culture 60–4
charismatic structure 62
religiously focused
lifestyle 64–70
trajectory of becoming
holy 70–2, 74–7
witness to the
Kingdom 15ff, 77ff, 84
history 36–43
institution 72, 114–19, 129
new realism 144ff
spiritual hungers 117–19,
121–39
state of perfection 148ff
Rigali, Norbert 104

Sachs, John R. 22
sacraments 129–30
sacred-secular 60–4, 150
Schnieller, Peter 32
Schroeder, Roger 34
Scott, Margaret 123
secular
buffered identity 19, 105
cross-pressures 119–20
enchanted-disenchanted 17–18
exclusive humanism 15–16, 19,
102, 112, 120, 155, 164
great chain of being 17–18
immanent frame 17
indicators of secularity 14–21,
155
instrumental reason 20
maximal demand 81–4